A BREATH AWAY

John Strouse

A novel based on true events

AUTHOR'S NOTE

A Breath Away is an autobiographical novel based on true events and events believed to be true, such as dreams and apparitions experienced by the author. In some cases, information received during apparitions was condensed from several visitations to maintain the continuity of the story line.

DEDICATION

This book is dedicated to Kyle, my grandson. Sadly, Kyle was stillborn. Holding Kyle at birth would have to suffice for hello, goodbye and a lifetime of memories. Everyone has a story somewhere deep inside. For a time I had been pressed by some unseen force, an inner urging, to tell my story. In Kyle's honor and to give him some place of existence in our physical world, I have given Kyle my story.

ACKNOWLEDGEMENTS

Sincere gratitude to Victoria Vila, my editor. She made my story worthy of telling. Thanks to Laurie Hawkins for her encouragement and for having an open mind during initial consultations.

Thanks to my family and friends for their support. Above all, thank you to my wife, Adele, for believing in me.

Thank you to all those in spirit so frequently with me.

INTRODUCTION

This is a story of dormant human ability. This is my story. It spans more than 50 years. The only reason I remember it is that my deep-seated insecurity kept me alert, but I never fully understood what was happening as I walked through my own life.

I believe that I have been directed to tell my story because many people are having so-called paranormal experiences involving spirit communication. Yes, contact from the Other Side.

What if you could be more aware of the workings of your own soul and the guidance that is available to you, just for the asking? You could participate more fully in the unfolding of your life. You would discover that paranormal experiences are actually misunderstood latent abilities. Explore further and you will find more confidence, self-acceptance, love and happiness. This is real. See for yourself. I wish you peace on your journey.

Blessings,

John

"The caterpillar dies so the butterfly could be born. And, yet, the caterpillar lives in the butterfly and they are but one. So, when I die, it will be that I have been transformed from the caterpillar of earth to the butterfly of the universe."

—*John Harricharan, author and lecturer*

PROLOGUE

Winter 1957

Like a blanket of fog, an eerie hush descended on the second grade class at Saint Rose of Lima Elementary School in West Philadelphia, a mixed socioeconomic section of the city. Tension in the room was ratcheted up several notches, a state usually reserved for a visit from Mother Superior. Everyone without exception was stiff-backed and saucer-eyed, watching the top student standing at the blackboard and stumbling to find the answer to a simple math problem.

Sister Mary Callistus was out of patience. Three other students, chosen to demonstrate addition and subtraction at the board, had already solved their problems and returned to their desks. Now, only Kyle remained.

"We will stay here until this problem is solved, even if it means we all miss lunch," announced Sister in her most stern voice.

Kyle, already a much too reticent child, drifted deeper into his trance. No one was aware that, just that very morning before school, Kyle's lifelong canine companion was killed in a bizarre traumatic accident. The dog, a German shepherd, originally named Gretchen but recently renamed Yeller after the central character of Kyle's favorite book "Old Yeller," was part of the family even before Kyle. The two were returning home from their morning walk. Yeller was off her leash.

In the middle of the narrow street, the local bread truck that served the majority of homes in the area was stopped with the engine running, as was the custom. The bread man would run up the steps of his customers' houses with his basket full of the day's bread and extra offerings, hoping someone would come to the door or had left a note for an additional item. Since it was early in the day when the bread truck came into Kyle's neighborhood, the bread man would never knock or ring a doorbell, but just drop off the bread and hope for a note.

Kyle was passing by the truck as the bread man stood in the back rearranging his basket items. Yeller ran across the street, then turned back to wait for Kyle, who was beginning to cross the street. At the same time, the bread man moved quickly from the back of the truck into the driver's seat. Unaware of them, he threw off the parking brake and gunned the engine, propelling the truck forward with a lurch.

Yeller sensed the imminent danger and in one magnanimous gesture, leaped at Kyle, paws at chest height. Kyle fell backward, landing hard on the curb he had just stepped from. Yeller was less fortunate. As she lay lifeless on the street, Kyle knelt by her side, sobbing. The bread man ran to Kyle's house to summon help and apologize. When Kyle's Dad approached the scene he shouted, "Men don't cry! Go off to school!"

Now Kyle, as he stared at the board, was repeatedly seeing Yeller, seemingly full of life, running toward him, beginning to jump onto him. Each time just before contact, the vision would disappear and the blackboard was visible again.

Kyle cocked his head to the right. He hadn't realized Sister Mary had moved to within an arm's reach behind him. Out of nowhere, a thunderous slap to the back of his head sent it forward, crashing into the blackboard with a thud. Stunned, humiliated and afraid, he wanted to cry. Instead, he reached up and wrote the number nine just below the smudged eight.

"It's about time!" Sister barked. "You must be full of the devil today! Class, get ready for lunch dismissal."

All the kids put on their coats and found their places in line while Kyle, his eyes to the floor, avoided any interaction. It was six long blocks to his house and he would have to hurry to eat and be back to school on time. It wasn't until a half block from school that the daily procession, boys first, two by two, then girls in the same fashion, would feel comfortable enough to mix together.

"Did it hurt?" The soft tender voice came from behind. Kyle turned to see the new girl.

"Yes, it did, but it's okay."

She reached out and wiped his forehead clean of a faint number eight.

"There, that's better."

"Thanks," Kyle said. "Did you just move here?"

"No, I came from Sister Marie Claire's third grade class. I've been out sick a lot and they decided to put me back a class so I wouldn't fall behind."

Just then a shiny black car pulled to the curb and

stopped where the two were walking.

"It's my mom," she said. "Hi, Mom, why are you here?"

"You and your friend get in and I'll explain to you."

The two children entered the car.

"This is Kyle, mom."

"Pleased to meet you, Kyle. We will drop you off at your house. Is it near here?"

"Just drive straight until Louis's grocery on the corner, we live on that street," Kyle said.

"So, let me tell you why we're here," said the girl's mother. "Doctor Green called and you have been accepted as a candidate in their new hospital research facility in Chicago. We have to start on Monday. The hospital has found a furnished apartment for us while we're there."

"Chicago? Oh Mom, I'm tired of all the tests at different hospitals. I'm tired of all the doctors. I miss my friends." She began to cry.

Kyle, feeling a great empathy for his newfound friend, moved closer and put his arm around her. The mother turned to face her daughter, leaned over the front seat and stroked the girl's hair.

"Now, now, your Dad and I are tired too, but we're not giving up on you. We are leaving for Chicago tomorrow and will be staying as long as we must. We have arranged for a private tutor for you and since you are doing so well with your piano studies, we are getting you a new piano in Chicago. We'll have it shipped here when you're well again and we return home."

Her tears diminished. She held Kyle's hand tight and he could feel, but not understand, her desperation.

"Louis's grocery, here it is," the mother announced.

"I hope you get better real fast and hurry back," Kyle said to the girl.

She leaned toward him and kissed him on the cheek.

"I'll see you again," she said, "I promise."

The car stopped and Kyle exited. Suddenly he turned to her and said, "Hey, what's your name?" As the car slowly pulled away, she leaned out the window and shouted, "It's Hannah!"

The back of Kyle's head remained sore for several days and that night, the dreams started. At least Kyle called them dreams as he told his father about Yeller visiting him while he was sleeping. Then there were the others, people whose identities were unknown to Kyle. They were dressed in all sorts of strange clothing. Some women wore black sparkly dresses and danced on tables all the while smoking very long cigarettes. Men with them were dressed like penguins and would dance the same dance but never on the table. One night, as Kyle was playing with Yeller, a man appeared who called himself Gramps. He rode on a horse-drawn wagon full of bottles arranged neatly in wooden crates. He offered Kyle and Yeller a ride and as they traveled through the dream, Gramps introduced Kyle to Grandma Wilhelmina and the twins.

When Kyle told his father about Gramps and Grandma with the 'Will-something' name and the twins, a sadness never seen before came over his father's face. Kyle thought he was about to cry, but tears were a stranger to the man whose cheeks stayed dry as desert dunes. Instead he threw up his hands and shouted, "Listen, men don't dream! Men don't cry! Men just work!"

The dreams stopped.

THE MEETING

March 19, 1969

Kyle began his cross–campus dash. He hated this day. He hated every day. The dreaded uneasiness was beginning to build again inside his stomach, confirming to him that he didn't fit in, he didn't belong. This inner fear was a daily occurrence.

"Jesus, 11 o'clock already," he mumbled under his breath as the Temple University bell tower sounded the time.

"Look out, soldier!"

That shout prompted him to jump back onto the curb as a speeding car whizzed by.

"Warmonger!" That insult came from inside the car as it missed its intended target by the narrowest of margins. Or did it? Kyle had felt something strike his chest and left forearm. He looked down and noticed a smashed egg where he had stood moments ago. Another hit the brass button on his jacket and broke, spilling its contents at the point of contact, leaving him looking rather ridiculous. He wanted to shout "Thank you" to the anonymous voice of warning in the crowd waiting to cross Broad Street, but he was too humiliated.

Soldier, he thought. If they only knew his deep and hidden feelings. Joining ROTC, the Reserve Officers' Training Corps, was his father's idea. At least he assumed it would have been his idea had they ever had that conversation, or any exchange for that matter. Theirs was more of a silent relationship filled with tense moments and unspoken words, which led to misconceptions. Kyle felt he wasn't the son his father desired.

Every Wednesday, ROTC members were required to wear full dress uniform on campus and participate in classes at the armory, a foreboding fortress from another era right there on Broad Street, a main artery in Philadelphia. In better weather, marching drills and ceremonies were held on the university's sports fields, a brisk seven-minute march from the armory. Kyle, his curly brown hair cropped neatly, was in uniform returning from a memorial service commemorating the death of an ROTC graduate.

An especially vicious war was taking place in some far away country, Vietnam. Half dozen years earlier, no one paid much attention to that area of the world, but recent times were different. The war was foremost in the mind of every male between the age of 18 and 26. For that age group, the country had a policy of involuntary induction into the service, the draft. If you were in college, you were exempt from being drafted and the fears of being called to war. College enrollment was up.

Vietnam was the first war ever televised on the network evening news. Seeing the carnage every day just after supper was hard for the country to stomach. The unpopularity of the war brought out the worst in some. Just seeing a military uniform on campus was enough to spawn an impromptu protest. Kyle considered himself fortunate to have avoided

8

being the target of any such protests, until today anyway.

Early the previous school year, Kyle's freshman year, the lieutenant colonel in command of ROTC at the university discovered Kyle was majoring in music and that he was proficient on the trumpet. Since then, he was required to play Taps at all the memorial services, which were becoming increasingly frequent.

Ironically, Kyle was comfortable playing Taps to honor the fallen soldiers. As he played, the somber, mellow notes wafted across the open fields toward the houses of the surrounding neighborhoods, creating an echo, a haunting repeat. Kyle imagined the accumulated notes taking wing, escorting the very soul of the deceased soldier and carrying him through the hearts of his parents one last time, on a journey to freedom from the agony of war, from earthly pain – a final flight of liberation. Kyle thought he could release the parents' sorrow and the departed soul at the same time, taking them to a better place as the simple notes drifting toward heaven dissolved into nothingness. For once, Kyle felt he had a place.

As Kyle raced to the College of Music, he detested the time he would waste finding a practice room, especially now with everyone working on their mid-term performance piece. Who would design a school of music without ample practice rooms? He desperately needed to practice, not for any particular course, that was useless as his grades were in free fall, but for an opportunity to record the song he was just about finished writing. A friend from high school was completing a recording-engineer internship at a local studio and was permitted to bring reputable local talent into one of the older studios on Sunday mornings to gain some additional experience. Kyle welcomed the opportunity to put a small group of musician friends together to make a demo tape of his song.

When Kyle arrived at Presser Hall, Elmer, the guard, was dutifully opening the door and greeting all the young women entering the College of Music. Everyone was younger than Elmer, who tried to look smart in his uniform that came complete with a nightstick as the single line of defense.

Elmer was short, extremely thin and just plain old. He seemed so out of place in a security position. Earlier the previous month, it was discovered that Elmer had been unwittingly helping young women exit the building and load large musical instruments into their waiting vans, except none of the women were students and none of the instruments were ever seen again. Now, Elmer awaited his fate, apparently unaware of any disciplinary action.

Inside the building, Kyle expected to see a throng of people madly searching for an available practice room. Much to his surprise, an empty room was waiting right on the first floor. He knew not to question such luck and took it as some sort of sign as he piled in with his trumpet and secondhand attaché case of manuscript paper. As he closed the door and settled in, Kyle sensed something special was about to happen, despite all the rushing, the grieving parents at the memorial, the constant threat of violent protests and the ever-present inner fear.

After 30 minutes of working on his song at the piano, Kyle felt a deep sense of accomplishment. It was the kind of feeling he was familiar with only when music was involved. He had thought that music was his future, but the other students looked askance at him in class. They laughed at his lack of real musical knowledge. Twelve years in Catholic schools that did not have a complete music curriculum left many blank spaces in Kyle's knowledge of musical theory, but the inner hunger to perform had carried him so far. However, the difficult classes this semester were forcing him to reevaluate his choice of music as a career. If this one song could just be a hit.

Kyle began to drift into a daydream of imagining what it would be like to write a song that made the charts when someone entered the room.

"Oh that's right," he mumbled, "not a star yet. I'm sorry, is my time up? I didn't realize we had limits. I apologize for taking so long."

"Relax," said a young girl with a light tan complexion. She walked toward him while she extended her right hand saying, "I'm Hannah."

Kyle managed a smile and introduced himself while grasping her hand, which had a noticeably soft touch. Hannah spotted his trumpet.

"Hey, you play the trumpet? All I've been hearing since you came is the piano."

Kyle was confused. "You've been listening for the last half hour?"

"I'm in the room next door, been here for a little while."

"What's that?" Kyle gestured with his head and eyesight in the direction of Hannah's left arm. Her arm was supporting and concealing some sort of rectangular box.

"It's a Ouija board."

There was a tremendous feeling of calmness about her, some kind of reverence emanating from her. For a brief moment, Kyle sensed a sort of familiarity but then was distracted by her beauty. He was kind of liking Hannah and he desperately needed a friend at this time in his life. Maybe this chance meeting could lead to a date, at least. He never had a steady girlfriend. He spent his teen years hiding behind his trumpet.

"I'm sorry," he said, "it's just that I never heard of uh, whatever it was you said."

"O-U-I-J-A-B-O-A-R-D," she spelled out each letter. "It's used to communicate with the dead. I can't believe you never heard of one of these before."

"No, I haven't," Kyle said. "I never thought of talking to the dead. Why would you want to? I don't think it's possible. I was raised a Catholic and we don't talk to the dead, uh…unless of course they're a saint and we want a favor or something like that."

Kyle was thinking about this for the first time, but his religious upbringing supported the idea of not asking questions, just following the previous generation.

"Well, what do you think happens when you die?"

Hannah asked. "And don't say heaven or hell."

"Oh, is there another choice?" Kyle answered. "I was hoping to go to that Big Band in the sky. You know, all the greats will be dead by then and we'll just spend every day playing the charts."

"No really, what do you think happens?"

"I never really thought about it. I don't know that I have to be concerned just yet. I think I have plenty of time before I meet my maker."

Just then Kyle had an inward vision, it was the strangest of things. He saw himself as a soldier and sensed he was no longer a student. He was trudging through some very dense forest, sweaty and nervous. Suddenly, a round of gunfire rang out.

Kyle snapped back to the present with a jerk of his head and a short but intense inhale. Then an unexplainable deep sense of curiosity came over him.

"Hannah – please tell me about that board. I'm ready to listen."

"Kyle, I'd be happy to!"

Hannah removed the Ouija board from the end of the narrow box. It looked about the size of the Parcheesi game board that Kyle was familiar with, only it didn't unfold to double in size. She looked back into the box again as if something were missing.

"Come on out," her words broke the somewhat awkward silence. She then removed an odd-looking plastic heart-shaped object with a clear disc in the center of the pointy end.

"This is the planchette."

Again, Kyle noted an air of respect or reverence permeating the room. Maybe it was a call for him to pay attention.

"With this," stretching her arm in his direction, "we can see the words, one letter at a time."

She placed the board on the piano bench. They positioned themselves on opposite ends of the bench and knelt on the floor. She rested the planchette on the board's surface.

"First, I'll say a prayer." She didn't bless herself, as was Kyle's custom, but simply spoke in free verse.

"Sarah, we come to you today for guidance. Please demonstrate the existence of the spirit world to Kyle. Above all, Sarah, keep us safe."

Keep us safe? Kyle's mind cautioned. He didn't dare say anything but a very soft "Amen."

Hannah told him to place his right hand gently on the planchette, at the wider end.

"Keep your arm elevated," she said, "to allow for freedom of movement." She did the same.

She leaned forward toward Kyle and for a moment he thought she was going to kiss him over the length of the piano bench, but then she said she would keep track of the words, one letter at a time.

"Just wait, Sarah will let us know when she's ready."

"Who exactly is Sarah?"

"Sarah is my spirit guide. She's been with me from

birth. She keeps me safe and leads me to the things I should be lead to."

"Oh, like a guardian angel?"

"Exactly, only she's not an angel. She lived on earth some time ago and is now helping me through guidance. That's why she has the name spirit guide."

"What happens to your guardian angel?"

"We really don't have a personal guardian angel, just spirit guides. Somehow the terminology got interchanged and mixed up through the years."

Just then the planchette started an arching motion across the board, left to right then back again. Finally, it settled on the letters. Hannah kept track.

"K-Y-L-E, your name, C-O-N-F-I-D-E-N-C-E; confidence. I don't get it."

Kyle was getting it. Confidence was his weak point. He had spent most of his life self-conscious and withdrawn. For a number of years, he was considerably overweight. The ridicule and exclusion he experienced from his peers led to a life on the periphery, in the shadows of the other students. Music was his way of expressing himself – his trumpet was his voice. Everything he wanted to say was hidden in his music.

After high school graduation, on a dare from his sister, Kyle enrolled in a martial arts course at the local Y.M.C.A. During the summer, he lost 40 pounds. He started college as a new person. From the outside, his 5'8" frame agreed with the weight loss. His self-esteem should have been coming alive, but it wasn't that simple. When he looked in the mirror, what he saw was the old Kyle. To make matters worse, after the weight loss, a spinal irregularity became noticeable. A curvature, probably from birth or shortly after, had gone undetected by doctors in the 1950's and overlooked altogether with the extra weight he carried. This defect was never addressed.

"N-E-W-B-E-G-I-N-N-I-N-G; new beginning. Wait!" Hannah exclaimed as her hand left the planchette. "We need some paper to write this down. This could be lengthy."

Up to now, Kyle wasn't checking the letters on which the planchette was stopping. He really wasn't sure if Hannah was making up the letters or forcing the planchette to stop over those particular letters to spell a message she could use to control him. He did not feel any sense of uneasiness though and wanted to trust her. He searched through his case to find the single sheet that wasn't manuscript paper and handed it to Hannah.

"Okay, let's continue," she said. "Sarah, are you there? Sorry for the interruption."

"That's okay," Kyle said.

"No, I'm talking to Sarah," Hannah chuckled.

They began again. This time Hannah put her left hand on the planchette so she could write with the right hand. Kyle leaned a little more forward to see the letters himself. Sarah appeared to have returned and the planchette began again by arching across the board as if searching.

"Q-U-E-S-T-I-O-N; question," said Hannah as the letter indicator stopped. "I think she wants us to ask questions.

She's done this before."

"Ask if I have a spirit guide."

"Of course you do," Hannah replied. "I'll ask the name."

"What is the name of Kyle's guide?" she directed her voice to the board.

"G-L-A-D-Y-S; Gladys, your guide's name is Gladys!" Hannah nodded emphatically.

"Wait a minute!" Kyle exclaimed. "My guide is a woman? I got stuck with a woman? That explains a lot!" Kyle was thinking about his lack of interest in sports. But then he thought that maybe it was all a mistake. Perhaps Hannah had gotten a wrong number and wasn't talking to Sarah at all. Hannah could tell he was uneasy.

"I think we should end this for today," Hannah said. "Sarah, thank you for the information, I think." She glanced at Kyle. She returned the board to the box, then the planchette and paper. Standing, she turned toward him and moved closer. Her voice was softer now than before. "I'm so glad we were together today, Kyle. Don't worry about having a woman for a spirit guide. I'm sure she'll bring much sensitivity to your life."

Then, ever so gently, she kissed him. It was the softest kiss anyone had ever graced him with. He was mesmerized. Before he could take action, she had turned and was headed for the door with that board under her arm, looking much the same as when she had come into the room.

Kyle's heart started to race. He quickly ran toward the piano, ripped the corner from a sheet of manuscript paper and grabbed a pencil. He never before had the courage to ask a girl for her number on the first meeting, he always left that for the second meeting. There never were any second meetings.

When he turned back, she was gone, but the door was shut and he hadn't heard it move. Kyle's heart beat faster. He ran into the hall to find her but no one was in sight except two students sitting on the floor.

"Which way did that girl go? She was carrying a box under her arm."

"We didn't see anybody," one responded, "are you done with the room yet?"

Remembering he left his trumpet unattended and the recent rash of missing instruments, Kyle abandoned the idea of looking further and returned to the room disappointed.

No use in remaining now, he thought. He had tried returning to the piano to complete his song, but thoughts of the time he had spent with Hannah overtook his mind. Of all the events that morning, the idea of not seeing Hannah again seemed the most devastating. *How crazy,* he thought, *I don't even know her. Come to think, I never even saw her before and I've been here almost four semesters. As attractive as she is, I would remember that face. She is a student here? Yes, she said she was working in the room next door. She didn't carry an instrument with her? Must be a piano major.* He gathered his belongings and slipped out of the room, down the hall toward the front door and past Elmer, who was standing with one foot propped on a chair talking to a young female student.

Kyle's car was parked about two short blocks away.

Parking was always a problem on campus if you wanted your car nearby. If you were fortunate enough to find on-street parking, chances are your car might not be there when you returned. Today was a lucky day, he thought as he approached his 1956 black and white Chrysler New Yorker. This 13-year-old beauty took a while to pick up speed, but once that happened, *"Look out, she ain't a stoppin',"* he recalled the words of the elderly gentleman who sold him the car.

Kyle piled his things into the car and drove off. It was a beautiful day with the feel of late spring, rather warm for March. He noticed quite a few school-age children playing on the sidewalks and darting into the street and realized they must be off this afternoon. He pointed the car in the direction of Broad Street to avoid them, although it usually meant more traffic. Kyle had just enough time to get home and out of his ROTC uniform, practice his trumpet lesson and get off to work. He was a part-time waiter at a popular restaurant called the Italian Villa and rarely spoke to anyone about the job.

Kyle had the windows down and was mentally reviewing his song creation in an effort not to think about Hannah or Gladys. The warm breeze allowed him to relax and enjoy this time driving. Traffic was fairly modest and it looked as if he was about to get really lucky today. He was making a series of green lights that would allow him to drive nearly two miles without stopping, unheard of in most of the city. The street had the appearance of being wide open since the road was bordered on the east by a rather large cemetery. It even had a lengthy curve to the right and there was no traffic light around the bend. Some excitement never hurt. If you let your speed build to 50, the two miles were yours for certain. Kyle stepped on the gas: 35, 40, 45... a little more gas – 50!

The air felt good and surprisingly fresh as it gusted past his face. The car sped forward and for a moment life was good. He could see nearly two blocks ahead and all systems were go. Kyle thought of the astronauts. They were planning a moon landing or something this summer. He pretended to be an astronaut, feeling the amazing force at the wheel. *We're going into uncharted territories now,* he thought. *Look at those craters! Oh no,* with a bit of disappointment, *it's just abandoned houses in North Philly.*

Kyle could see the light a block and a half away changing to red. Traffic ahead was coming to a stop. The open area of the cemetery had long disappeared and Broad Street had turned into Roosevelt Boulevard, an enormous 12-lane roadway. Each set of three lanes was separated by a tree-lined grass median. Houses occupied both sides of this thruway. Plenty of pedestrians were out and about. He shifted his foot from the gas to the brake.

"No, wait!" he shouted.

He tried again. *No brakes!* His mind screamed. He repeated the motion several times. "Where's the brake pedal?" he shouted.

Traffic was stopped a block ahead now and Kyle was still moving at 50. He switched from the center lane to the left lane and at the same time pulled up on the parking brake. Nothing! No decrease in speed at all. Was this some sort of bad dream? His mind raced with all sorts of scenarios, none of which had a happy ending.

Closer now, he saw only two choices. Hit the car directly in his path and for certain hurt whoever was in it, or drive up onto the grass median and deal with hitting one of the massive trees and probably be killed. Kyle was choosing the latter when, out of nowhere, he saw a mother pushing a carriage with another child walking beside her, right at his estimated point of impact with the tree.

"Shit!" he screamed, "I can't take a chance."

With the sea of brake lights ahead, it was obvious even in his state of disbelief that a catastrophe was only seconds away. The New Yorker, Kyle and anyone in their path seemed to be headed for a tragic rendezvous. Kyle surrendered to the inevitable, closed his eyes, braced for impact and shouted, "Gladys — help me!"

The day was clear and warm. The dampness of perspiration seemed to be everywhere. What had taken literally seconds seemed to be stretched into an immeasurable amount of time. *Where's the noise,* he thought, *the sounds of crunching, twisting metal, the screams? Where's the pain? Oh, this must be the moment of death when your soul leaves your body and dissociates from all earthly feelings.*

"Look mommy, he fell asleep."

Those words brought Kyle back to reality. He quickly opened his eyes and to his utter amazement, saw the New Yorker resting three feet behind the stopped traffic. What had happened? He turned his head to the left and saw the mother with carriage and boy in tow. They were standing just beside his open window but still on the tree-lined median. The boy's eyes and Kyle's were on the same level. He wanted to ask them what had happened, but they hurried in front of the New Yorker to catch the remaining few seconds of the red light, apparently oblivious to what had transpired just moments ago.

The light was changing now to green as each car waited its turn to go. It wasn't until his turn to lunge forward that Kyle realized his foot was still on the brake pedal, which was totally depressed to the floor. He decided one potential disaster was enough for the day. He shifted to park and reached through the window to wave the traffic around. When the traffic cleared, Kyle and the New Yorker limped to the right side of the road. He found a phone booth and made two calls, the first to the auto repair shop that his dad used to ask about a tow truck. The other call was to his mother, to have her call Celeste, his closest friend from the restaurant, to ask if she could pick up his change of clothes for work because he'd be catching a bus straight there. He also told her one more thing since she would probably be in bed when he arrived home, "Mom, Happy Birthday."

That evening at the restaurant, things were exceptionally busy. Because Kyle arrived late for his shift, his entire station was filled with other servers' customers. He would have to help speed things along to clear his tables so any subsequent customers, and their tips, would be his. He was eager to recount his story to a fellow worker but there just wasn't time. He mentally reviewed his near accident, searching for clues about what stopped his car. Toward the very end of the night, Celeste offered him a ride home. Kyle seized the opportunity, not only to get a ride but also to tell someone else the story, to hear the words of what happened spoken out loud.

In the car, Kyle asked Celeste to take the long way to his house and he would tell her a very unusual story. She did and he began, starting from earlier in the day at the College of Music. He spoke of the practice room that seemed to be waiting and about Hannah and the Ouija board and Sarah. He couldn't remember who exactly Sarah was, only that she was not living. He told her Gladys was another one of those invisible people, only she was assigned to him. Just then a chill shot up his spine. Goose bumps appeared on his arms. Excitedly, he turned toward Celeste.

"I was wondering how my car went from 50 miles an hour to a complete stop, just like that. The last thing I remember saying is, 'Gladys help me!' So what do you think, Gladys stopped my car? Oh wait, I didn't even tell you about my car."

"That will have to wait till next time," Celeste interrupted. "Someone needs a good night's sleep, that's what I think!" In the excitement of his realization, Kyle hadn't noticed that they reached his house. Again, he returned to reality. He thanked Celeste for the ride and left.

In the safety and solitude of his bed, Kyle reviewed the sequence of events one final time. *The car was speeding, no way to stop. I petitioned Gladys; the car stopped.*

"No wait," he said softly. Then in thought again: *the car was speeding, no way to stop; imminent death or maiming; petitioning for Gladys' help; the car stopped. Did a miracle happen? Did Gladys save my life? Why is it so hard to accept? What really happened?*

Kyle was on his back facing the ceiling and thought it wouldn't hurt to show some appreciation.

"Thank you Gladys," he whispered. Then the strangest sensation came over him. The very top of his head seemed to be vibrating, but inside. He touched his head and didn't notice anything unusual. As the feeling continued, it intensified, causing a slight dizzying effect.

Kyle continued to whisper, "Gladys, if you are out there, could you maybe stick around? I mean, if it's not too much to ask – I need you."

DUTY CALLS

Kyle arrived on campus the next day wearing civilian clothes. Everything was different in civilian clothes – no demeaning profanity, no second glances. He traveled from the bus stop and headed for his only class in the College of Music. Arriving at Presser Hall, Kyle first passed Elmer and then the practice room from the day before, which was occupied. He wondered if Hannah might be in there, but then he heard the distinct sounds of an oboe. On his way to the second-floor classroom, he ran into a friend who told him the class was cancelled but the midterm would be Monday. That was all he had scheduled for the day.

With his newfound free time, Kyle decided to look for Hannah. He would first go to every practice room that was occupied. If he heard anything but a piano, he would skip that room. For all the other occupied rooms, he would open the door and pretend as if he had mistakenly entered the wrong room. Forty minutes later, no luck. He asked a few of the female music majors from the dorm if they might know Hannah – again, no luck. With only days left until semester break, Kyle was desperate to find her. He had one last idea as he was leaving, to ask Elmer. Why not? Hannah was certainly attractive enough for Elmer to acknowledge. If anyone knew her, it would be Elmer.

Kyle realized that in all his time there, he had never in fact spoken to Elmer. He found himself clearing his throat to get Elmer's attention away from the passing group of female students. Elmer faced him now and asked, "You want something?" Part nervous and part embarrassed, Kyle mentioned he was looking for someone named Hannah, a student here.

"I don't recall a Hannah. Are you sure that's her name?"

He thought for a second and answered yes, he was sure. At that, Elmer reached for a briefcase. From inside he produced several sheets of paper stapled together. Looking around, he handed them to Kyle.

"Here's a list of all the College of Music students. Don't tell anyone, but after semester break, everyone will be issued an ID card and number, something about instruments missing. Stand here and look at it, take your time, just don't let the dean see you if he walks by."

Kyle was surprised by Elmer's response. He took his time and examined each name carefully.

After a few minutes, he was ready to give up. With despair in his heart, he returned the list to Elmer.

"Any luck?" Elmer asked.

"Afraid not," Kyle said, his voice wavering. "It's okay. Thanks anyway."

"Reminded me," Elmer continued, "I had a granddaughter named Hannah. Passed away a few years back from some kind of cancer. Played the piano and was a natural at it. She hoped to come to this school. That's why I took the job as a guard here when I retired from the Fire Department.

Her parents lost everything traveling around the country looking for a cure. This school gives a large discount to families of employees. She's gone, but I just can't seem to retire again. Working here and seeing all you young people keeps her alive in my memory, I suppose. Let's see, she might have been around your age." He paused and extended his fingers as if counting. "Yep 20, would have been 20."

"Well, thanks again."

"Hey, you know what's funny?" Elmer began again. "I swear I saw her walking down the hallway yesterday. I turned away, thinking my eyes were playing tricks on me and when I turned back, she was gone."

"Yesterday?"

"Yep. Around this time."

Kyle had to get some fresh air and left abruptly, although he couldn't imagine any more information coming from Elmer. On the bus home he was really confused. Had Hannah been something his mind created? Did he hate life so much that he was having a breakdown? What about Elmer's sighting? What about the Ouija board? That certainly seemed real. And what about Gladys and the failing brakes? Who stopped his car the day before? Too many questions, but no answers. Kyle decided to reach out to someone who had seemingly helped before. For the remainder of the trip home, he prayed to Gladys for guidance.

* * *

The days slipped by and the semester ended. Whenever Kyle thought of Hannah, it just made him confused and depressed. He had hoped for a sign from Gladys by now. Two months had gone by since he prayed to her on the bus. He also was confronted with the truth about continuing with school. His grade point average was so low and the classes next semester were even more difficult, why continue?

Until now, Kyle was protected from the draft because he was a college student. However, something called a lottery was replacing the draft at the end of the year.

The lottery system used birthdays. On December 1, 1969, numbers were to be selected and assigned to each day of the year. Beginning January 1, 1970, if you had a low lottery number, you would be notified to report for a physical and ultimately be inducted into the Armed Forces. A higher number assigned to your birthday and the chance was good of never serving. The first year of the lottery applied to all men born between January 1, 1944, and December 31, 1950. In the succeeding years, just men 19 years of age would be eligible.

Although the war in Vietnam was still intense and Kyle was born in 1949, he dropped out of school, got a job and took a chance with the lottery. When the dates were picked, Kyle's birthday was assigned a very low number. Three months later, he received a letter from the Selective Service System to report for his pre-induction physical.

As the day of the physical approached, Kyle's anxiety grew to an almost overwhelming point. He remembered the ever-so-brief vision from when he first met Hannah, of him trudging through a dense jungle surrounded by devastating fear, the vision that caused him to listen to her. Was that Vietnam? Was it about to unfold?

Two nights before the scheduled physical, he had a very peculiar vivid dream. In it, he was standing on a street corner and a dull olive-green bus was traveling down the street. The bus pulled up to him and stopped. The door opened and the driver turned to look at him and flashed a big smile. The door closed and the bus continued down the street without him. The especially odd aspect was that the driver was an older woman wearing army fatigues and though she passed him by, her smile seemed warm and inviting.

Kyle decided to take public transportation to the physical since it was in town and parking was scarce and costly. Frankly, he felt too jittery to drive. He was well aware that the casualties in Vietnam from his high school, Father Judge, were mounting exponentially. He felt he was not immune to a similar fate. In his mind, this day was a matter of life and death.

As he rounded the corner to the building where he was to report, he saw the bus from his dream parked on the sidewalk. Written on the side in black lettering was Department of the Army. He thought of the dream and knew there was a message in all of this, but there was no time to think.

In room 108, when Kyle presented his Selective Service card at the check-in station, he was told to remove all of his clothes but underpants and put his shoes back on after removing his socks. He was issued a new set of papers.

"Here's a locker key for your belongings, get a move on," the sergeant said.

Kyle wondered if he would be going home that day at all. From there, maybe you just get on the green bus and that's it – there is a war going on after all. In the next room, he met up with the main body of young men being examined that morning. After 45 minutes of prodding and poking, of blood samples, eye exams and urine testing, the group was told this would be the last station.

"If you made it this far boys, you're ours," thundered a husky male voice from the corner of the crowded room. "Okay everybody, bend over." Kyle obliged.

Maybe it was the stress of the day or the desperateness of the situation, but Kyle suddenly felt filled with an inner laughter. It was the kind of laughter that, if it escaped to the outside, would be uncontrollable. He felt a tap on his shoulder.

"Son, come with me."

Shit, he thought, *how did they know I was laughing inside?* Someone grabbed the papers he had accumulated at each station.

"Bend over for Dr. Myers," came what he thought was his first official command as a soldier. Again, Kyle obliged.

"Okay, you can stand up. Take these papers and your Selective Service card over to that station and they will mark it 1Y. Your spine is just too crooked for our needs. It's called scoliosis. Get your clothes on, lunch is being served upstairs."

He pointed the way to the next station. Kyle raced to the station of freedom, as he mentally dubbed it. At that moment, nothing looked more beautiful than that 1Y designation stamped on his card. He worked his way through the group, back to the locker, being careful not to make eye contact with anyone to avoid being told, "This was some sort of mistake, just get on the bus." He fumbled with his clothes but managed to dress in record time. Forget lunch, he thought, it's just a trap to change their minds when they see how much you eat. Kyle imagined a voice saying, "Eats okay, let's put him on the bus!"

In his haste and state of euphoria, Kyle became disoriented and lost track of the way out of the building. He spotted a person in fatigues mopping the floor down a deserted hallway. He approached the slightly bent figure from behind.

"Excuse me, I'm a little lost, which way to the street?" he asked.

Kyle gasped as the person turned to reveal the face of the woman from the dream, the bus driver. She smiled the same smile from the dream as she pointed down the hall. He wanted to take a moment to ask her who she was and if they had ever met – after all, she seemed so familiar – but just then, two officers turned down the hall and were walking in his direction. He reached into his pocket to reassure himself his Selective Service card was still there and decided not to press his luck any further. He headed down the hall and saw the exit sign. He turned to wave a silent thank you to the woman but she was gone. Odd, he thought, for an older person to finish that fast. The officers were still coming, so he hastened his exit.

"Whoa," he exclaimed as he entered the street right where the green bus was positioned. Kyle quickly did an about face and walked as fast as he could without attracting attention. It wasn't until he had walked halfway home that he felt secure enough to catch a city bus for the remainder of the trip.

THE WISH RESURFACES

August 1988

"There's quite a load here," Samantha said somewhat sarcastically as she looked around Kyle's almost empty apartment.

"Samantha, when my first marriage ended three years ago," Kyle said, "I knew someday I would meet someone, fall in love and get married again – at least, that was my heart's desire. I thought I could avoid the hassle of moving if I didn't have any furniture."

"Yeah, that and you couldn't afford furniture," said Samantha, Kyle's soon-to-be second wife. She was a petite, attractive woman wearing a modest amount of jewelry as part of her ongoing attempt to maintain her femininity within the budget of a bank teller. "What did you do with the little bit of junk you had?"

"Oh, I gave it to Pete from work. He's getting divorced and needed some lovely furnishings for his new place." They both burst into laughter.

"Hey," Kyle said, "maybe it'll bring him luck, I certainly was lucky."

"Kyle, a lot has happened in this little apartment."

"You're not kidding; I finished growing up here. I learned to accept myself, found you and fell in love." He turned to give her a hug.

This was Samantha. At 38, she looked younger than her years. They had met six months after Kyle's separation. She too came from an irreconcilable marriage, a relationship that left her with a woeful self-image. Kyle could empathize with that – feeling inadequate was the bane of his life. Samantha had built a wall around herself of anticipated mistrust in a new relationship but, through the time they had known each other, it seemed the wall was dismantled brick by emotional brick. They didn't do it consciously, it just happened.

Now, Samantha looked at Kyle through very understanding eyes. She knew he had nothing in a material sense, but she saw in him an intense hopefulness for the future. In exchange for her love, she wanted only loyalty and about this, she was adamant. Kyle never spoke of Gladys to her even though Gladys had become a mainstay in his life and he felt her presence every day. He wanted to share Gladys with Samantha, but felt it was just too precarious a situation. After all, how could he explain something like the car accident that never was? How could he explain the thoughts that came into his head out of nowhere? Accompanied by the head vibrations, they were clearly not from his own mind. But mostly, he could never explain the love he held in secret for his unseen companion, nor would he want to. He would never hurt Samantha that way. Her trust in him was fragile.

In Kyle's first marriage, after the birth of their third and final child, the visitation dreams of his youth had returned. This time, the people and colors in the dreams were much more vivid. Kyle was excited by the dreams, but his wife's response was one of skepticism and wariness. Looking back, Kyle thought maybe it was his irrational enthusiasm about the dreams that hastened the decline of the marriage. Perhaps he shouldn't have been so open in sharing those experiences. As the tension within his marriage intensified, the dreams diminished. Now, he was willing to abandon any curiosity about the dreams to prevent jeopardizing his relationship with Samantha.

"Hungry?" Kyle asked.

"Getting hungry. I told the girls we would be home for lunch."

"Here's some money, if you want to order sandwiches across the street, we can take them home. Ah, that sounds great – home. I can finish here, it won't take long."

As Kyle packed, thoughts of the past flooded his mind. While loading pieces of exercise equipment into the station wagon, he remembered the pain associated with the spinal surgery, after the 1Y Selective Service designation came back to haunt him. The pain started when the cast and body jacket were finally removed a year after the surgery, and increased dramatically as time went on. It seemed to signal an emasculating future for a man who prided himself on being the family's provider. When he moved to the apartment the next year, the image of dire years ahead along with the guilt of no longer living with his children was agonizing. He could have given up, but there was a glimmer of an idea off in some distant corner of his mind, calling to him. It was the promise of something better.

When Kyle would focus on the idea, searching for some clarity, the top of his head would vibrate intensely. For this reason, Kyle attributed the distant inspiration to Gladys. Their bond had strengthened while he lived in the apartment and illogical as it might sound, Kyle thought Gladys was prodding him to start an exercise program. He couldn't afford a gym membership, so he decided to work out in his apartment. He recalled how he selected the modest amount of equipment with his tax return and started on the road to his new beginning. He remembered how excited he was when the pain was half gone on the very first day of exercise and completely gone as the workouts progressed, how his inner fear subsided to a level he could deal with.

Kyle thought of all the conversations he had with Gladys in this apartment, all the while never knowing for certain if she were real or in his imagination. Of course there were the head vibrations that coincided with communicating with Gladys. He had come to think of them as a call to attention from Gladys and considered them to be some form of validating her existence. Gladys had impressed upon him that the way they communicated was called thought transference, exchanging information by means other than the known senses, though he would never relinquish the image of her speaking directly to him.

As moving day approached, Kyle had spoken aloud to Gladys on several occasions, asking her to please move with him. He felt their relationship was far from over, even though he was moving in with Samantha in anticipation of getting married. He promised Gladys to tell Samantha about her eventually.

"How much more Kyle?" Samantha's voice startled him as he was leaning into the car rearranging boxes.

"We're finished here," he said with a broad smile and somewhat teary eyes.

"Great, let's go home," she said as they held hands and walked to the open apartment door. He reached for the knob and giving it a good yank, turned toward Samantha and kissed her.

"Yes, let's go home."

∗   ∗   ∗

"Congratulations!" The Justice of the Peace handed Kyle and Samantha their marriage certificate. The ceremony was simple and blissful.

The next day they went to the mall to pick up some last-minute items for their combination vacation-honeymoon that would begin in two days. Having gotten to the mall a bit early, they went inside to wait a few minutes among the senior citizens walking their laps. As the stores slowly lifted their gates, they decided to go in different directions. Kyle would find Samantha in Macy's shoe department in 45 minutes.

As Kyle's second marriage was getting underway, he had an unexplainable deep yearning to follow some sort of spiritual path – not religious, but spiritual. Perhaps it is best described as looking for the God within. As he walked to the health food store, he suddenly felt the peculiar head vibrations and the determined presence of Gladys pushing him toward the bookstore, whose manager had the gate only a fraction of the way up. Kyle stooped low and entered the store practically on all fours. Gladys continued pushing until Kyle was in the back of the store in the New Age department. He stretched his right arm out straight, as he thought Gladys was instructing, and used a sweeping motion along the bookshelves, like searching for something in the dark. Finally, he was drawn to a thin book almost obscured by its surrounding neighbors.

"Predicting the Future with Cards," he whispered, "a system using regular playing cards, whereby a person can foresee coming events."

Well, that's a tall order for such a small book he thought. There was something familiar about this book. He was sure he hadn't read it, as it had just been released. After considerable examination, he bought the book and realized time had slipped away. He headed back to meet Samantha, but not before thanking Gladys for her involvement.

Kyle still wondered why this book seemed so familiar, like rediscovering an old friend. Then it dawned on him: the year 1975. It hadn't been a very satisfying time in his life. Married, with a second child on the way, he had just lost his job at a semi-trailer manufacturing plant because the trucking industry was cutting back. Caught up in a nationwide recession, he bounced from job to job. He needed to know there was hope in his future. Someone referred him to a psychic, Marie the Reader, and being desperate for news of better days ahead, he scheduled an appointment. The day came and he found himself on the doorstep of what seemed to be an ordinary house in an average neighborhood.

"Please come in," Marie had said. A comforting feeling emanated from the rooms as he walked to the combination kitchen-office. He noticed that the uneasiness in his stomach, which he lived with every day, had suddenly vanished.

On the kitchen table was a well-worn deck of cards, not tarot as one might expect, but ordinary poker cards. He sat at the table and Marie handed him the cards. He could see that her hands were as worn as the cards. He was instructed to shuffle the cards and cut the deck into three sections, leaving each section face down on the table.

While Kyle shuffled, Marie was busy in the kitchen. At the range, she stirred a large pot of what she called spaghetti gravy. Next, she poured two cups of coffee and placed one next to Kyle. She sat at the table, reached for each pile of cards and rearranged them as a whole deck. Then, she began to place each card on the table, face up in a semicircle. When 16 cards were used, she stopped. She studied the cards silently for a minute, stood up, lit a cigarette and started pacing. She began the reading.

"This is your life in the present. You were put here to heal others, but first, you must heal yourself. Self first, then others. You must acknowledge and make use of your intuition. When you do, your abdomen will stop hurting. It is the place of psychic energy in the body and yours is abundant but not being diffused correctly. In time, you will change this. There is a job coming your way. It will consist of unusual hours but be very secure."

When she finished giving information from the first layout, she gathered the semicircle of cards into the deck again and handed it to Kyle with the same instructions. She stirred the gravy and lit another cigarette. Then she laid out a different number of cards in a different shape and began again.

"This is your life in the future. There is a plan for you. There will be meaning and purpose to your life, but you won't see it until you are much older. At that time, a woman in white will be with you. I sense she is on the other side. She is whispering something to you and I am hearing the phrase 'lost secret.' I see her handing you a pen. She is encouraging you to tell others."

That was all he could remember her saying that day but that was enough. He did remember the feeling of hope he had as he sat in her kitchen, knowing that someday even his life, a life seemingly not well planned, would work out.

Oh my God, the wish! Kyle thought excitedly. *I made a wish that someday I could do the same, comfort and encourage others to continue on when life doesn't seem worth living.* Although his wish had been pushed aside in the gloominess surrounding unsteady employment, lost in his feelings of inadequacy in caring for his family and forgotten altogether in the turmoil of a marriage in decline, it still existed deep within. Kyle would return to the cards one day and now the cards were calling. If he had not experienced his own personal hardships, he may have never arrived at this point.

"Right on time," Kyle heard Samantha's voice from

behind. "I hope you found what you were looking for." He turned to greet her with a kiss.

"Yes, fact is, it found me."

*   *   *

For 13 years, Kyle had been working at a very mundane job. He had been employed since 1977 as a clerk with the United States Postal Service. Although not exactly his dream job, it did provide him the opportunity to feel secure and earn a steady income, just as Marie the Reader predicted. He was grateful for this.

Kyle had been hired for the overnight shift. To his surprise, he found that it was quite a busy time at his location, the main post office in Philadelphia. Despite this, the work was very repetitive and through the years became rather boring. To compensate for the boredom, Kyle had begun using the book on card reading at home in an attempt to see into the future.

For several months, Kyle heard from within himself a group of syllables sounding like kun-da-lee-nee. He didn't know what it meant or the correct spelling. He wasn't even sure if it was a word. He would hear it several times throughout the week. Even though it was accompanied with the usual head vibration, he thought it might be someone's surname from the mail he was sorting, a name he saw repeatedly that had gotten trapped in his subconscious.

Then one night, Kyle made a remarkable discovery. A co-worker was pushing a load of oversized mail, stacked haphazardly on a flatbed hand truck, toward Kyle for him to sort. The load got away from the co-worker and went crashing into a nearby safety railing. Oddly, only one magazine from the load of hundreds fell onto the floor. As Kyle retrieved it, he noticed the phrase "Kundalini Meditation" in bold print on the cover. He made note of the magazine, Mother Earth News. He also noticed his head was vibrating and he knew Gladys was involved in this somehow.

Across the street from work was a major train station that was also home to several restaurants and specialty shops. One shop was a bookstore that carried every magazine in print, if the owner's boasts were to be believed. After work, Kyle ran across the street to find the magazine. As he read the article about meditation and the life force energy known as Kundalini, he realized Gladys was encouraging him to embark on a journey into meditation.

Kyle began practicing meditation every day. As he did, he could see the similarities in quieting the mind during meditation and quieting the mind while performing mundane work. He realized he could find value in his routine job instead of frustration. While he worked he would quiet his mind and just let the random thoughts drift by without actively thinking.

This combined home and work meditation schedule seemed to help Kyle as he continued to read people's future in cards, expanding from his family to friends and then to anyone who even vaguely expressed an interest. Although his readings improved with the addition of meditation, he still didn't feel comfortable charging a fee.

Kyle continued to talk with Gladys. He noticed a

pattern to when Gladys would communicate with him, that is, to impress an idea or thought in his mind. It seemed to be while driving to or from work, while working alone or while exercising or taking a shower. Of course there were other times, but these were the most common. The vibration of the top of Kyle's head still accompanied each impression by Gladys and had become second nature to him. He referred to this as head-buzz.

One Friday morning, as Kyle traveled home from work, he had a persistent head-buzz and urge to call his cousin Grace, one of the women he had used to practice seeing into the future.

He called, but she didn't answer the phone. "Hi Grace, this is Kyle, sorry I missed you. I am getting the feeling I should call you. Maybe I'm supposed to give you a reading. If you're available tonight, let me know. It's the usual charge, free."

That night, as Grace met with him, he told her she was pregnant. With surprise, she said she had just learned of her pregnancy that morning but hadn't told anyone yet. He also saw the possibility of a miscarriage but wasn't certain he should alarm Grace with such dreadful news. It seemed to be connected with a flight coming soon. Kyle asked if she had a trip planned involving a flight. She confirmed she was scheduled to fly to Florida on Tuesday, just four days away, and was very excited about the trip. He made her promise to speak with her doctor before taking the flight, never mentioning what he had seen.

On Monday evening, Grace called to tell Kyle that when she spoke with her doctor, he said whatever you do, don't fly. As a teenager, Grace had been diagnosed with a bleeding disorder and was considered a high-risk pregnancy. She had been trying for three years to conceive and did not intend to jeopardize the pregnancy. Florida could wait. She thanked Kyle. He felt maybe there was some bigger purpose to receiving messages from Gladys and offering readings after all.

Two weeks went by, and on another trip home from work, Kyle kept hearing the word ectoplasm, accompanied by the head buzz. It was exactly the same type of prompt he had to call Grace, but without the feeling of urgency. He remembered how that worked out and did not want to ignore this. When he arrived home, he went to the encyclopedia to look up this vaguely familiar word.

"A cloudy, foggy substance seen during the materialization of a spirit entity," he read in a whisper. Although the encyclopedia continued with much more, Kyle closed the book, let it fall onto the sofa cushion, looked up and said aloud, "So?"

Since Kyle and Samantha's work schedules were opposite, he was accustomed to being home alone during the day and talking aloud with no one else in sight. Of course there was Gladys. He knew she was the one behind the message.

"So, Gladys, what is this all about? Are you finally going to reveal yourself to me?"

Look further, her message came back loud and clear within him.

Kyle reached for the book and found the ectoplasm page again. He read the page and continued, carefully at first so as not to miss a clue, but by the third page, he started to skim the paragraphs. He read an entry about the Society for Psychical Research in London, something about people from the 1800's.

"Okay, I'm finished, Gladys. What's the point?"

Go back, that's me, that's me, Gladys insisted.

Again Kyle returned to the book. He scanned the pages in reverse now and after turning the page back once, his stomach tightened when he caught sight of the name Gladys Osborne Leonard. It was listed with others as early members of the Society for Psychical Research started in England in 1882.

"Oh my God, Gladys, is that you?"

It is! It is! Gladys impressed. At that moment, the head buzz was very pronounced.

Kyle ran to retrieve the 'L' volume of the encyclopedia.

"Thank you so much, GLADYS OSBORNE LEONARD. Let's see what it says here about you. Now I can tell Samantha."

Kyle reached the LEONARD section of the book but to his surprise, no mention of Gladys. How could she be overlooked? She was mentioned in one book, why not the other?

"Okay, maybe it's under 'O' for OSBORNE."

Again, the search went nowhere. Discouraged now and noticing it was long past his bedtime, he wrote the full name on a small piece of paper and placed it into his wallet for safe keeping.

Kyle climbed the stairs on his way to bed so he could get up for dinner with Samantha, which was their custom. They both realized that if their marriage were going to survive their work schedules, they would each have to give a little. Since Kyle had the odd hours – working through the night, often six nights a week, with additional hours each day for overtime – he was more than willing to be flexible. He often recalled his father's words that men don't dream, they just work, and realized that he too worked entirely too much. In that respect, he had become much like his father, but he attributed it to being undermined by major spinal surgery and a long recovery and the threat of losing his house. He vowed to never be in such a financially vulnerable position again.

LOVE IS THE BRIDGE

One morning, upon his arrival home from work, Kyle noticed Samantha's car still parked in front of the house. After a brief moment of concern, he remembered she had an appointment for her annual physical.

"Are you okay? You look rather pale," she asked as she greeted Kyle with a kiss.

"I think I'll go right to bed. I am exceptionally tired and somewhat dizzy. I never felt this way before but I don't think there's any reason for concern. After all, I just had my annual checkup two weeks ago." He went to bed and fell into a very deep sleep; at least he thought he was sleeping. He began having a lucid dream.

In the dream, Kyle was in a windowless room. His attention was drawn to the right side of the room by an extraordinary bright radiating light. In the center of the light, there seemed to be someone dressed in an all white garment, similar to a monk's robe, complete with a hood. There was an overwhelming feeling of peace in this room. Kyle could see what seemed to be a person standing beside the form, but the brightness of the light made it hard to identify who it was. Kyle took two steps forward and so did the person beside the bright light. Tears welled in Kyle's eyes while an awkward smile stretched across his face.

"Hannah? Hannah is that you?" he asked, choking back tears.

"Yes, Kyle, it is me," she answered. "I'm here to take you another step on the path."

"But wait Hannah, I was looking for you. I went back to find you the day after but couldn't. I searched, really I did – I did, believe me. I, I..." his voice softened now, the desperation gone, "I miss you. You seem to have something I'm looking for. You know, I even went to that guard, I forget his name right now, to ask if he knew you."

"Kyle, do you remember when we first met?"

"Of course I do! I was just recounting the story of...."

"Kyle, think back further," Hannah interrupted, "we were both so young. Do you remember?"

"No, I don't think I do."

"This may help." She waved her right arm slowly through the empty space beside her.

"Yeller! Yeller!" Kyle shouted. "That's my dog, but she died when I was in second grade!" Yeller ran to Kyle and lay at his feet.

"That's right Kyle, think back to second grade."

"It was my worst day! My dog died, my dad scolded me for crying and my teacher slapped me at school. I was having such a terrible time," he paused, "but then I met a girl who was having a worse time."

"Yes, Kyle," Hannah said with a bit of mystery in her voice, "go on."

"That's right! She was very concerned for me over what had happened in class. Then I was compassionate toward her because she was terribly sick. Oh my! Hannah was her name also. You're the same Hannah?"

"Yes Kyle, I am the same Hannah."

"I'm confused."

"We lived in Chicago several years as part of an experimental program, which did extend my life in the physical. My parents had planned for us to move back home after high school but my body had had enough, I was weary and it was my time to cross over."

"So you were dead that day in the College of Music?"

"Yes, my dear Kyle," she laughed, "but it's not what you think. I am what you call dead right now, but I'm here, aren't I? I just don't respond with those on the physical plane in the same manner as I once did. I see my family and I am aware of them and what they are doing. Sometimes they sense my presence; unfortunately it makes them think of me with such sorrow and that in turn breaks my heart. I do appear occasionally in their dreams and that seems to be the best way to touch them, to tell them I'm okay and that I love them. Kyle, it's all done through the power of love."

Kyle stepped forward again and held out his arms, hoping to entice Hannah closer.

"We mustn't touch today, Kyle. We are in a state of purity. You see, when I crossed over, my parents were devastated, of course, but their continuous grieving for me kept me attached to the physical plane. Since I was fond of music and had looked forward to it as a career, when I crossed over, my parents donated my piano to the college of music I was planning to attend. It was there in the practice room that day. Some years back when everyone had been hopeful for a full recovery, my grandfather had promised to pay my tuition. He even took a job at the college. Since my beloved grandfather and piano where at the same place, it was only natural I hung around there. Then you came along, down on yourself and lonely, and I was able to help you find something better."

"You started me on my path."

"In return, you helped me.

"I did? How's that?"

"When I was ill, I looked so hideous. I wanted a boyfriend terribly, for someone to love me other than my family. I never experienced that until you came along that day in the College of Music. I know about you searching for me and I am deeply touched, still today as much as I was back then. Your effort to reach out did matter. The energy connected with your desire for me, freed me from my earthly bond and helped move me to another level on my path."

Just then, Yeller stood, jumped up on Kyle and gave him a doggie kiss. Then she ran toward Hannah, jumped into midair and vanished.

"You see, we're here to help each other," Hannah said. "We are evolving together."

The tears returned again to Kyle's eyes, but this time it was too much to hold back. He sensed their time together was ending.

"Please don't leave, please," he pleaded.

"Kyle, I'm never that far from you. Call my name or

think of me and know I am with you. I am always just a breath away."

Hannah extended her left arm in the direction of the bright white object.

"Kyle, today you will be shown the process you call death. Transition to eternal life is a more appropriate phrase." She turned to face the bright form.

"This is my dear, devoted grandfather, Elmer. He has been transitioning to eternal life this morning. I have come to meet him and comfort him during this process. Is the name familiar?"

"No, I don't think so…wait. That was the guard from Temple – Elmer!"

"Yes Kyle, Elmer is my grandfather. All of this I am sharing with you comes from within the plan of God; no one has been left out. You may not think of yourself as much but you are here with me today because of your caring, loving ways and because you asked for guidance. In time, you will share this day with many. Always remember, love is the bridge to where I am, the world of spirit."

With that, a rose appeared in Hannah's hand. She kissed it and tossed it toward Kyle. He caught it. Then Hannah, Elmer and the dream were gone.

When Kyle woke, he recalled vividly the dream and seeing Hannah again. He felt great, not like missing someone but of gaining an eternal love. He remembered her saying she is always just a breath away. He recalled the last thing Hannah said, before she tossed the rose – love is the bridge to the world of spirit.

For some reason, Kyle thought of Gladys and said in his mind, *"Gladys, if the rose Hannah gave me exists on your side, I'm giving it to you as a sign of my love. After all, she brought us together and she would want it that way."*

When Kyle came downstairs, Samantha kissed him especially long and exceptionally hard.

"Mmm, what's that for?"

"Don't play dumb with me," she said playfully. "Thank you for the rose! That was one perfect rose you left on my car seat this morning. There it is on the table."

"Oh, you're welcome," he replied after an almost noticeable lapse. He walked toward the flower hoping to conceal his utter amazement. He didn't dare tell Samantha about Hannah; he could never relate that story without the emotional attachment.

During dinner, Samantha moved the rose closer between her and Kyle. He wondered if she had just received an inaudible request from Hannah or Gladys to do so.

It made him feel unfaithful to think he had given the rose to Gladys without thinking to give it to Samantha. The rest of dinner was awkward for him.

THE SEARCH FOR JEANE BEGINS

For quite some time, Kyle was hearing from within the name Jeane. He had a strong sense it was a woman's name and he felt he had to find her, but where? At work one evening, someone had left a course brochure on a break room table. It listed various adult evening classes being offered at Temple University's Center City Campus, a satellite of the main campus where Kyle's spiritual journey began so many years prior. None of the accredited courses appealed to him, but one of the noncredit courses looked interesting. It was titled "Metaphysical Awareness" and would explore the unseen world, touching on meditation, chakras, lucid dreaming, angels, guides and more. Kyle thought this would be an opportunity to meet others who might be having similar experiences.

Kyle registered for the class and soon found himself returning to a university setting. The instructor seemed straightforward and professional and he immediately felt at home with the material. The first handout pertained to meditation and chakras, which he was familiar with from the Kundalini article in the magazine, but this was much more in-depth. The next handout discussed guides and angels, which struck a chord with him.

At the last class, the instructor made available a list of practitioners offering astrological charts, tarot and intuitive readings, Reiki and mentoring. Three practitioners had the name Jeane, each with a different spelling. Could one of these be the Jeane he was searching for?

Kyle decided to call each Jeane to possibly schedule an appointment or at least chat a moment to perhaps pick up a vibe. However, each time he was supposed to leave a message, a strong sense of confusion would cloud his mind and he couldn't speak. He tried a second time to call each with the same result. Finally, as he meditated before going to work, he got a clear message from Gladys: *She will be on the other side. Be patient.*

Then one afternoon in January, as Kyle was finishing his workout on the equipment in his garage, he suddenly felt ill. He lay on the bed until Samantha came home.

"You're burning up." She went for the thermometer. "Oh my God, 104! You're on the way to the hospital!"

After a lengthy time in the emergency room, Kyle was admitted for a kidney infection. Antibiotics were administered, but the infection remained. He underwent tests and procedures of all sorts. Finally, it was decided to use one of the strongest antibiotics in the hospital pharmacy. By the end of the week, Kyle was on the road to recovery.

It was Friday night and Kyle was experiencing a rather peculiar, but vaguely familiar, feeling of light-headedness. Earlier in the day, the doctor had said he was doing well, so he wasn't alarmed by his dizziness. Since he still had a slight fever, the doctor was keeping him in the hospital. Kyle felt fine, just a bit dizzy and tired. It was late, so he decided that perhaps sleep was the best remedy. He closed his eyes and fell into a deep sleep.

At some point during the night, he was in the transitioning room from before, where he had met Hannah. This time he saw the bright shining shrouded figure, but no one else. Kyle had an awareness that someone was passing, or as Hannah had taught him, transitioning to eternal life, but no indication of who. Again, there was an overwhelming feeling of peace permeating the room.

"Kyle, move closer." A female voice came from the luminescent form. Kyle obliged. "Tonight, we will experience transitioning together. This is a beautiful process."

"Am I dying?" Kyle asked anxiously.

"You will be returning to the physical plane, but you will be transformed. Beginning tonight, you will have greater understanding, tolerance and empathy for those in the physical. Beginning tonight, you will have keener awareness and sensitivity with the world of spirit. You are here tonight because you have completed your surrender."

"Surrender? I never gave up!"

"Not giving up, Kyle. This is about surrendering your ego. Each of us must step from behind our mask of false pride and realize who we truly are. Only then are we free from the seduction of the physical plane. The need to surrender the ego is the reason for experiencing time in the physical. Surrendering is our redemption and our liberation. Now, let us begin."

With that, the form and Kyle began to shrink in size and transform into dime-sized, multidimensional star-like objects, brilliant like platinum but with awareness.

"Oh my God, I'll be pushed aside and lost for certain now!"

"We are part of a bigger picture that will never be complete if but one piece is missing," said the form. "No one is forsaken."

Then, the room changed to an open space that seemed to go on forever. In the space, Kyle saw an infinite amount of similar star-like objects, each one connected to the ones around it with brilliant narrow beams. Kyle became part of the immense network and began to resonate with the feeling of love, but on a grand scale. It was an intense emotional connection. He thought to himself: *We are connected, we are one.* With that thought, he returned to his physical appearance and was back in the transitioning room again. It seemed that when he thought of all humanity being united with a single consciousness, he had gotten the message and came back.

The mysterious person returned to her shape also. It was then he realized he still had no idea who this was. She must have read his mind, because at that very instant she said, "Someday you will deliver a message of great importance. I will be with you. I will help you prepare the message and in return, you will help me. Bringing forth the message will be the realization of my surrender, something I was unable to complete while in the physical. You will know when you are ready. Just say my name, I am Jeane." With that, the apparition ended.

When Kyle woke in the morning, he was certain that in time, it would all make sense.

It was Saturday and Samantha was coming to spend more time with Kyle. She was bringing pizza from their favorite place to share for lunch in the family gathering room at the end of the hall. Kyle was eager to tell Samantha about the dream, but realized he would have to water it down somewhat to make it more palatable. So he did tell her, but left out the part about the future message he was responsible to deliver. Also, he decided to use this time together to tell Samantha the whole story of Gladys and Hannah, from the very beginning, whether she believed or not. It just felt right.

When he finished, her response surprised Kyle. She said as he was telling his story, she was having hazy, fleeting memories of her maternal grandmother, who lived with Samantha and her parents. She had died when Samantha was 7 and had been sick and inactive for her last year, so Samantha's memories must have been from preschool age.

The recollections were of neighbors and occasional strangers coming to the house to have Grandmom take an evil spell away. She would sit at the kitchen table in front of a large bowl of water and a small bowl of olive oil. She would dip her right index and pinky fingers into the oil, then hold the fingers over the water, dripping the excess oil into the bigger bowl. Next would come either a gasp or a sigh of relief and always a prayer in Italian. Afterward, the water would be tossed into the back yard, along with a small handful of salt. She couldn't remember if her Grandmom accepted money for this service, but there was always plenty of respect and gratitude expressed.

After she told her own story, Samantha kissed Kyle.

"Thank you for being truthful," she said. "We have too much history together to walk away now. I suppose we'll just have to see where this takes us, but I swear Kyle, if you start with the olive oil and Italian prayers, I'm out the door!"

* * *

Early Monday morning, an elderly man came into Kyle's hospital room pushing a cart of assorted items for sale: newspapers, magazines, combs, playing cards, peanut butter crackers. The man said, "Want anything, buddy?"

"Philadelphia Inquirer, please."

Kyle glanced at the headlines in the newspaper and then turned to the obituaries. For some reason, whenever Kyle had the local paper, he was drawn to the obituaries. Maybe it was a good thing that hospitals were noisier than anyone desired, Kyle thought, especially with the full nursing staff returning from the weekend, because when Kyle yelled, "Sweet Baby Jesus!" no one seemed to hear him and no one came running. He reached for the phone and called Samantha.

"Honey, remember the dream from Friday night that I told you about on Saturday?" His voice was hurried and he didn't wait for a response. "Jeane Dixon died!"

Unfortunately, Samantha wasn't certain who Jeane Dixon was and couldn't quite get on board with Kyle's enthusiasm. He waited momentarily and then realized his dream didn't hold the same meaning for outsiders, though he never thought of his wife as an outsider. He hoped that someday she would at least acknowledge some of the synchronicities that he was experiencing.

In truth, Kyle wasn't all that familiar with the life of Jeane Dixon either. He knew she was a psychic who brought the idea of seeing the future into public view when she supposedly predicted in 1956 that a Democrat would be elected president in 1960 and would die in office. After President John F. Kennedy was assassinated, her fame skyrocketed. Kyle also knew that Jeane had written several books, none of which he had read.

Later that morning, as Kyle reflected on Jeane, he started getting a clear message that these dreams, visions, inner impressions and heightened intuition were part of his personal spiritual journey. Any support he needed would come from the other side, the side of spirit. He made a pact with himself that, despite anyone's lack of enthusiasm, including Samantha's, he would continue on his path.

Early Wednesday morning, the doctor entered his room saying, "Kyle, I have good news. You're out of here." Kyle called Samantha to pick him up.

Laughter filled the car as Samantha drove more carefully to avoid any bumps so as not to shake up Kyle's kidneys. This was her prescription and it was fine with him.

BREAKTHROUGH – 1999

In the summer of 1998, Kyle and Samantha had moved to a new development in the suburbs of Philadelphia. It consisted of smaller townhouses and condos and didn't attract families with children. Kyle continued to use the cards to see into the future for others. After his encounter with Jeane, the readings began to unearth deeper levels of information with specific details for his clients. To an outsider, it may have sounded implausible, but the results were so accurate, people began to praise his ability. Kyle decided to charge a small fee and save the money. In October of 1999, Samantha's employer was making personal computers available with an extended payment plan. They took advantage of the opportunity and bought their first home computer using Kyle's savings and the finance plan.

It was Halloween, and after dinner Samantha was going to her daughter's house to see her eight-month-old grandson in his first costume. From the previous Halloween, they knew no visitors would be knocking for treats, so Kyle, off from work that Sunday night, stationed himself upstairs assembling the computer components. Surprisingly, it was together and operational in no time.

Kyle sat at the desk staring at the monitor, wondering what he should do first. He clicked on the icon for the Internet provider and followed the instructions to go online.

"I would like to do something significant, at least the

first time I use this thing."

At that very instant, *Look up my name* entered Kyle's consciousness along with the familiar head buzz.

"Gladys, you're here?" Kyle said aloud.

Look up my name – Gladys, and after a brief hesitation, *do you remember the rest?*

The voice of Gladys was within Kyle, clear and forthright this Halloween night. He ran to the dresser where he kept his wallet. He searched for the small piece of paper on which he had written Gladys's full name. Kyle's heart sank with the thought that the set of encyclopedias where he had first found her name had been given away when they moved.

"I found it!"

He unfolded the paper to reveal her full name and carefully typed one letter at a time into the search box. Kyle had no idea what to expect on this first computer exploit. He clicked the mouse.

There before him was the picture of a woman with the caption: GLADYS OSBORNE LEONARD. Kyle froze in the chair. His heart raced. The shock of seeing his closest friend for the first time was overwhelming. He began to cry. The journey, begun in that college room with Hannah in 1969, had come to a significant juncture on this night. He wept the tears of 30 years, thinking of all the hardships he had shared with Gladys, never knowing if she were real or if he was insane. He thought of all the times he had asked Gladys for guidance, for confidence, for consoling and for the strength to continue his soul's journey – to find his purpose. The more he thought, the more he wept.

"Why didn't I look for you sooner? I'm so very sorry."

Kyle regretted not looking more diligently for Gladys, but his research skills were minimal; he never had access to a computer. Besides, he had been working close to 60 hours a week, so there wasn't time. Down deep he knew truly why he hadn't researched her name. He liked talking to Gladys and never wanted to chance discovering that she was a figment of his imagination. With tissues and tears everywhere, Kyle wiped his eyes and began to read the biography of the woman that appeared before him.

In the black and white photo, Gladys seemed to be in her early 40's and fairly attractive in a dark dress and a lighter colored shawl that covered her shoulders and draped down beyond the bottom border of the picture.

The biography explained that Gladys was born Gladys Osborne on May 28, 1882, in England into a financially successful family. At a very young age, she experienced spontaneous visions of other places, such as fields of flowers, which she would describe to her family. She was instructed by her father never to speak of such things and she obeyed.

In her teens, the family went through a difficult financial period and Gladys had to fend more for herself while the family fortune dwindled. She worked in the theater in London singing opera, acting and dancing in shows. As she moved into her own, she slowly began to regain the extraordinary ability she had experienced as a child.

One weekend, while her mother was sick, but

seemingly not seriously ill, Gladys was staying at a friend's house. At 2 a.m. she was awakened, as she described, with a vision of her mother in the center of a very bright circle floating a few feet above her. Her mother looked several years younger in the vision and Gladys sensed she was at peace and safe. Later in the morning, Gladys was summoned to come home; her mother had died at 2 a.m.

Gladys later met an actor, Frederick Leonard. They became best friends and eventually married. She had an inner yearning to explore the fundamentals of Spiritualism and psychic ability. She met two other women working at the theater with the same nature as her, that is, curious about the world of spirit. Together they began to communicate with the deceased using a technique called table tipping, asking questions of those who had passed.

"What, no Ouija board?" Kyle remarked, as he recalled Hannah and him that first day. "Hey wait! Gladys, remember that day when I met you? Do you know Hannah? Have you ever met Hannah?" He waited for a reply, but none came. Kyle continued reading. Eventually Gladys connected with a spirit guide named Feda, who told Gladys she would be used to demonstrate mediumship to the world. In time, Gladys became a trance medium and was one of the most tested mediums of the 20th century. Until now, Kyle had never heard of the terms medium, trance medium or mediumship.

The biography went on. Through her lengthy calling as a medium, Gladys had garnered the admiration of England's notables, both in scientific and socialite worlds. She was honest and dedicated to her work. On March 10, 1968, Gladys Osborne Leonard passed quietly at the age of 85.

Kyle was beginning to cry again. Just then, he heard noises from downstairs. He moved across the room to shut the door, and then turned to face the monitor again.

"Gladys, I truly love you," Kyle said aloud just as Samantha called from below.

"Anyone home?"

"I'm upstairs, I'll be right down," he said, putting an abrupt ending to the tears.

Kyle touched his index and middle finger of his right hand to his lips and gently kissed them. Stretching his arm in the direction of the monitor, he touched the screen and Gladys's picture with the kiss.

"Good night, I'll see you tomorrow."

He shut the computer down and darkened the monitor, hoping he could repeat the process and find Gladys the next day. He looked toward the ceiling and half smiling said, "Gladys, I'll see you whenever you want. Please stay with me."

Kyle didn't tell Samantha about seeing Gladys on the new computer. He didn't want to diminish the emotion of the evening. Instead, they talked quietly about their evenings. Samantha shared photos of her grandson's first Halloween. Kyle told her that the computer was up and running and asked if she had any ideas for what to do with it. Then, since it was a rare occasion that Kyle wasn't working, they retreated first to the sofa with a glass of wine and conversation, then to the bedroom for much more.

THE DEMONSTRATION

Through the years, Kyle always worked the late shift. He would return home around 9 o'clock in the morning. Of course, he would have to sleep in preparation for the next night's work. On Saturday mornings, since he was off that coming night, he was accustomed to sleeping just three hours. One particular Saturday, he woke with one thing on his mind. As he went downstairs to make coffee, he made note of a mild head buzz. Then he told Samantha about his desire.

"I've got a strong urge for Chinese takeout."

"Sounds good," Samantha agreed. Later that afternoon, they went to their favorite Chinese restaurant. On the way out, Kyle noticed a stack of thin magazines advertising local resources and events of a holistic nature. He took one and put it in the bag. After dinner, Kyle made coffee and held the two fortune cookies, offering first choice to Samantha. Then, just as he picked up the local ad magazine, the phone rang. As he reached for the phone, the booklet fell back onto the countertop. When it fell, it flipped open to an especially colorful ad.

"Hello – hello? No answer, probably a wrong number." He examined the caller ID screen.

"Nothing on the caller ID screen. Never saw that before."

"Maybe it's Gladys," laughed Samantha.

Kyle's attention was on the booklet. He reached out to

bring it closer while he read: "Mediumship demonstration, connect with your departed loved ones. Come be a part of an exciting evening with Dr. Simone to witness the connection with loved ones who have crossed over. Space is limited, reserve early." He turned to face Samantha. He had a sober look about him. "You know, that just may have been Gladys who called. Maybe she was behind everything that transpired since I woke up – my strong urge for Chinese food, finding the magazine and now calling to have us stop and look at the ad. It fell open on the counter, right to the ad, when the phone rang."

"And…maybe it's just a coincidence," Samantha added.

On Monday morning, Kyle registered for the mediumship demonstration by phone. He was really looking forward to the evening, but because he was wary of a scam, he told himself to show up that night with an open mind.

Finally, the evening was at hand. Kyle arrived at the one-story office building trying to hold back the feeling that something exciting was about to happen. After all, he wanted to be fair and impartial in his evaluation of the evening's events. The name *Quest for Learning* was artistically painted on the front window and a placard of the same was attached to the front door.

Kyle sat in the reception area and pretended to read a magazine. In truth, he was observing anyone who told the receptionist they were there to attend the demonstration on mediumship. It turned out that only a small percentage of people were there for the demonstration. He heard registrants for cooking class and beginners' art, as well as an upholstery class and square dancing. He made note of four people who had not pre-registered but signed up and paid at the door. Especially noticeable were two women, the first of which said to the receptionist, "My sister and I would like to sign up for the contacting the dead class, if there are any openings." They were accommodated and took the last two seats in the small reception area. The time to begin was approaching, yet all the participants were still seated in the reception area.

"The mediumship demonstration will begin shortly," the receptionist announced. "Simone is in the room conducting a private session. When she's finished, you can enter."

Five minutes later, the classroom door opened and two people looking to be in their mid-60's came out. The man walked on ahead while the woman appeared to be wiping tears from her eyes. Everyone waiting in the small area had turned his or her attention to the two newcomers. Very impressive, Kyle thought, if this is an act to pique our interest, it seems to be working. A third person then exited the room, a woman in her early 40's, he guessed. The first woman suddenly stopped and turned to face the second. She extended her right arm and what started as a handshake instantly evolved into a hug.

"Thank you again so much, Doctor Simone. You've given us the hope to go on. God bless you." She turned and left. *Oh, they're really good,* Kyle thought. *Could this be the first sign of deception?*

Simone walked to the receptionist, whispered something and then headed in the direction of the restrooms. The receptionist announced to the group, "The demonstration will begin in 10 minutes. Please have a seat in the classroom."

As the group of nine filed into the classroom, they noticed seats arranged in a semicircle. Among the group, seven were women; Kyle was one of two men. Simone entered the room and right away put them at ease with some type of invisible energy.

"Good evening everyone, my name is Simone. I'm sorry I'm running late but I had an unusually long session just before. That couple you saw lost a family member suddenly and very tragically. They needed to connect for information with the hope of finding closure."

"How long ago did the person die?" the woman in the second seat asked.

"The family member crossed over three weeks ago, very tragically."

"Murder or car accident?" asked the man in the first seat.

"I've already told you too much, confidentiality you know, but I do want you to realize how valuable mediumship is, so let's just say very suspicious circumstances and leave it at that." She shifted her weight, turned around as if looking for a blackboard behind her and then faced forward.

"Now tonight, oh wait, thank you for coming! Did I say thank you for coming yet?" A few heads nodded. "Tonight, I will speak about mediumship in the first part of this demonstration. The second part will be connecting with departed loved ones who have come here with you tonight. Has everyone heard of mediumship?" No hands. "Anyone?"

Kyle had read the word mediumship online in Gladys' biography, but he wasn't going to be put on the spot to explain what he knew, so he just ignored the question.

"How about if I say channeling, anyone ever hear of channeling?" Simone asked. Heads started nodding and everyone raised their hands.

"Channeling is a more current term today, but the original term is mediumship, which I prefer using. By the way, I neglected to say I have a Ph.D. in psychology. I'm only telling you because I am constantly walking a fine line between my professional stature and mediumship, the off-the-beaten-path modality."

Simone went on to tell the story of mediumship and how it began in the United States in 1848 and grew in popularity in the early 20th century, specifically in the second decade during World War I. However, with the surge of fraudulent practitioners, the hardships of the Great Depression, World War II and the arrival of television, mediumship gradually diminished in the United States. Recently though, there had been a resurgence of channeling or mediumship, in which she was happy to be involved.

She continued on until the first half of the evening was over and a short break was offered. So far, Kyle could detect nothing dishonest in her delivery.

After the break, the class returned to their seats for the

real reason everyone had come, to connect with departed loved ones. Simone had moved a chair to the middle of the semicircle during the intermission and was now dimming the lights. She sat facing the group, took a slow deep breath and seemed to transfer her consciousness to some distant place.

"Let's begin. There is a young male, a teenager, age 17, standing next to you." She pointed to one of the sisters sitting next to Kyle. The woman started crying and nodded her acknowledgement. Simone produced a box of tissues and began passing it to Kyle's neighbor. When Kyle turned to hand the tissues to her, he noticed the other sister was crying equally as much.

"He took his own life three months ago. He wants to apologize, realizing now how devastating his actions were to you. He also wants to warn his best friend that they are not dreams he is having of him, but real visitations. His friend is about to start taking medication because of these occurrences. His parents think he is traumatized. Let me see if I can get some names here. Billy is the deceased boy and his friend is…um…an 'R' name is the best I can see right now."

"All of that is very accurate," said one sister. "Are you certain he is next to me?"

"Yes," said Simone.

"The peculiar thing is, Billy is my nephew." She reached her left hand out and placed it on the knee of her sister, "My sister is Billy's mother."

The group did a collective gasp.

"We always were very close," continued the tearful

woman, "I'm his godmother, and whenever his mother, well…my sister, would yell at Billy, he would come over my place. We live across the street."

"Oh, I see," said Simone. "I believe he is too ashamed for what he did to approach his mother." Simone looked toward the mother to include her in the conversation. "What about the friend, does he have a friend with an 'R' name?" The sisters looked at each other and simultaneously said, "Ricky!"

"If you can talk to Ricky's mother, tell her the dreamlike visitations will stop and hold off on beginning the medication, it may affect on her son. Can you do that?" They agreed to speak to Ricky's mom.

Kyle lost track of the next few minutes. In his mind, he was repeating what had just transpired so as not to forget the sequence. Did the aunt give up any information during the reading? He didn't think so. The mother barely said anything. The tears seemed real and the fact that the aunt was sitting right next to him took away any question about using a caustic substance to bring tears forward. Thinking that perhaps he was being a bit too cynical, he reminded himself that he was just trying to be an impartial observer.

By the time Kyle mentally rejoined the group, Simone was talking to a woman three seats away from the sisters. He thought she must have spoken to the two women between, but he wasn't certain.

Simone pointed to the woman and said, "Although you're very young to have a deceased mother, there is a woman standing beside you that is claiming to be your mother. Your mother is deceased?"

The young woman nodded as the box of tissues started to travel in her direction.

"She is telling me she passed from cancer. Now, she is showing me something like a movie of what appears to be a manufacturing plant. Cigarettes are being made in this plant and she is spraying something in the production process. It is this substance that caused her cancer. She wants to tell you not to worry about getting cancer; it was from that spray, nothing genetic. She knows you are especially concerned right now because your daughter is the age you were when your mom passed. Is that accurate?"

"Yes, thank you, thank you."

"Oh, she's saying also, you are very sad that she never saw your daughter. She wants you to know that she saw your daughter before you did. She is closer than ever to you."

Simone continued, "You can see that your mom is aware of your concern about getting cancer, she really is very close to you. Talk to her whenever you want." *Talk to her whenever you want,* Kyle thought, that sounds like Gladys and me.

Simone pointed to the other male in the room, at least the other living male. She started with, "I see a partner here beside you. This is a romantic partner, is it not?" The man nodded. She continued, "He's sorry he had to leave so soon, as you know he was very ill. He wants to caution you though, about a decision you're about to make. He does not trust the man you are considering going into a business type partnership with. He is telling me that you also have reservations about this individual. Is that accurate?"

"Yes, very."

"Good! Someone different will come along shortly that will be more appropriate for your business. He says also to tell you to stop driving so fast." With that, the man began to laugh, which spread across the room just in time to lighten things up.

"That's incredible! I got a speeding ticket on my way here tonight," the man said.

Simone's attention was now focused on a woman on Kyle's right, two seats away.

"Your aunt is here," she said. "She lived by herself and was never married. Correct?"

"That's right," said the woman as she looked for the whereabouts of the tissues.

"She is saying that she regrets not doing enough in life. Not exploring the things she was interested in, not going out enough, being afraid, staying in every night after work and not finding a love interest. She could have done more – much more."

"Right on, that was my Aunt Mary," said the woman. "Her nickname was scary Mary."

"She looks to you now and is saying don't be like her. Take a chance in life, follow your heart. Just know that she is around you from time to time and is supportive of what you do." Glancing at her watch, Simone now directed her attention at Kyle.

"There are two people behind you, a man and a woman. The woman is telling me they are the grandparents

73

you never knew, however, they knew you from the beginning. The man, your grandfather, is now showing me something he made from smaller pieces of wood. It is the only remembrance of him that you have. Is this true?"

Kyle was trying to be expressionless.

"Yes, it is accurate. Please go on."

"Your grandfather, by the way, you look a lot like him, he is saying that your knee has been bothering you. Take the pills from the brown bottle. Your grandmother is talking again. She is saying she is your influence when you cook. Do you like to cook?"

Kyle was persuaded there was something to it all. He felt free to speak and confirm what Simone had said.

"Yes, indeed my knee is hurting. I did buy a food supplement, in a brown bottle, but have been neglecting to take it. I do cook frequently and love to experiment. I always feel like someone is standing next to me in the kitchen suggesting different ways to do things. Finally, there is something my grandfather made from wood. It's an old-fashioned baby's cradle on rockers. It is entirely made from pieces of wood that have been glued together. It's very unique, a real antique. We used it for all of our children. It is a very lovely remembrance from my maternal grandfather."

"I'm sorry, what is your name?"

"Kyle."

"You see, Kyle, how your grandparents are aware of the day-to-day events in your life? The cooking, the pain in your knee, even the color of the bottle of supplements indicates their awareness and involvement in your life." Kyle nodded silently.

Simone then addressed a petite woman with a very fit-looking body but a face that seemed beyond her years. This was the last person in the group. Kyle became lost in thinking of what he would tell Samantha about his reading and the appearance of his grandparents. When he came back to the moment, Simone was saying, "What we need to realize is that those in spirit are with us not in memory or imagination, but really present. You just can't see them that easily. With a different way of thinking, some training and practice, more people would be able to see the world of spirit."

She glanced at her watch and announced, "Wow, where did the time go? I'm sorry we ran over, but as you can see, this is an important issue to all of us. Let's all take a deep breath. Exhale, and again. Good! I want to make sure everyone is awake and able to drive home safely." Most of the group hugged Simone as they left. Kyle was last to leave and he too faced Simone and exchanged a hug.

"Thank you for such an emotionally charged evening. You really have demonstrated there is more to life and dying than we have been led to believe. Where do we go from here?"

"Funny you should ask," Simone said. "Earlier today I decided to offer a hands-on class sometime in the next few months. When I have it ready, I will advertise it. Until then, here's the name of a website you might explore." She handed Kyle her business card, on which she had written the URL.

When Kyle arrived home, Samantha was still awake

and she listened attentively as he talked about his evening. She did admire that he could remain excited about life, although she was doubtful of his direction and wished his interests were more mainstream.

"Well, I have to get to bed," she said.

"I think I'll spend a few minutes on the computer, that is, if you don't mind?"

"No, not at all," she said, relieved but a little guilty. They kissed and went their separate ways.

In the office, he booted up the computer and tapped out the URL on the keyboard. "This looks familiar." He was at the site where he had originally found the biography of Gladys, but he had never explored it further. Kyle ordered a manual on mediumship and noticed one more interesting offering. The author of the manual would tape a session of himself contacting the spirit of a deceased person anyone requested. He wrote a quick note stating he would like Gladys Osborne Leonard contacted and included the fee of $35.

"Let's see what someone else picks up," he whispered to Gladys, "maybe an outsider will confirm I'm not totally crazy." With that, he said good night to Gladys and joined Samantha in bed.

THE ROAD LESS TRAVELED

Two months had passed since the demonstration of mediumship. When Kyle picked up the current *Creative Wisdom* magazine, he saw the ad for the next event with Simone. The class would be held at the same place and the class members themselves would be contacting the other side this time. Kyle registered and looked forward to the opportunity for some hands-on experience.

Soon Kyle received the manual on mediumship that he ordered. After reading it, he decided to get more serious about meditation. He doubled his meditation practice time: once in the morning upon arriving home from work and again in the evening before going to work.

Kyle was able to sense main events in the lives of several of his co-workers before they began to unfold. He was always cautious about snooping psychically into someone's private life, but occasional spontaneous visions and impressions were unavoidable.

One of these co-workers, Marissa, was a displaced federal employee who transferred to the Postal Service when the Defense Department downsized and closed the Philadelphia Navy Yard. Kyle admired several of her qualities, particularly her soft-spoken personality and the fact that she didn't need to constantly be the center of attention. Perhaps because of his appreciation for Marissa's persona, Kyle began experiencing precognition of events in her life. Of course, he would never tell her anything he knew or thought he knew. He would, however, give a full report to Samantha during dinner when such an event was revealed to him.

Some of the events Kyle foresaw troubled him. When he saw Marissa about to get engaged, he was happy for her. However his body, or more precisely his gut, the ultimate gauge of the truth, told him otherwise. On the day of her wedding, Kyle received the mental message that she would be divorced before her first anniversary and this troubled him. When he told Samantha, she insisted it was nonsense, that Marissa and her husband looked happy together and they deserved every chance to be married without some gloomy prediction of their future. Eleven months later, Marissa's spouse filed for a divorce.

Soon the class with Simone was at hand. Kyle stole a moment to ask Gladys for any help she could offer. He had felt her presence in the car and thought he had seen, in his peripheral vision, an outline of her sitting in the passenger seat, but when he would turn to focus intently on her, the vision wasn't there.

Simone stood before the class of six. She gave a brief description of mediumship and mentioned that this evening they would experiment in connecting with the spirit world. She then seated herself off to the left, facing the small group.

"For the first hands-on exercise tonight, I need a volunteer to stand in front of the room." Kyle offered to go first. "Face the class. Elevate either of your arms parallel to the floor and lift your hand as if you're motioning someone to stop. Now Kyle, move your arm so your hand faces each class member. This is called scanning. Stop when you feel you should, then look in the direction of that person and experience what unfolds."

As Kyle stood, a great sense of calm came over him. He slowly began to scan the five women and sure enough, his hand felt compelled to stop at the fourth woman. Her name was Alyssa. She was younger than him, he guessed around 35.

"Here, this feels different."

"Now put your arm down," Simone said, "just relax; look to the left, then to the right of Alyssa. Look just above and beside her. Tell us what you see. Just relax and be patient."

"I see something," Kyle exclaimed in a whisper. "It looks like a circle of light. It's getting bigger and appears to be moving forward toward us, almost like the headlight of a train getting closer and closer."

For a number of years, Kyle had been having spontaneous visions, mostly while reading someone's cards. Of course they were visions of future events and possibilities, not discarnate entities. From those experiences, he had learned to keep any internal excitement to a minimum. Too much exhilaration seemed to stop the vision. He would communicate the visions during readings exactly as he saw them.

"Are you planning to travel, maybe a train is involved for a portion of the trip?" he asked. But before she could answer, he gasped. "It's changing! The circle of light is cascading down and the form of a woman is coming forward as if from the light. Hey, did I see this in 'The Wizard of Oz'?"

"Stay with it Kyle, just relax," Simone interrupted. "Now, along with what you see, what do you feel?"

"I feel warmth, not temperature warmth, something more of a welcome home warmth – the feeling you have going back to the house where you grew up, on Thanksgiving – the smells from the kitchen mixing in the air, the warm feeling from the family. Oh, it's the feeling of a family member!"

"Good," said Simone, "focus on the feeling associated with the woman. Can you sense her relationship to Alyssa?"

"Mother," he announced without hesitation. Shifting his gaze, he glanced at Alyssa, "Oh, that can't be, you're much too young to have a deceased mother." Just then Alyssa started to cry.

"But, I do have a deceased mother."

"Kyle, stay with it, just report what you see and feel. Don't think!" Simone instructed in a noticeably firm tone.

"She is telling me, although I can't hear the words, more of a knowing."

"That's thought transference," Simone interrupted, "mental telepathy, go on."

"Thought transference," Kyle spoke softly. He remembered Gladys telling him that too, quite a few years ago. He took this as a signal that Gladys was there. He was certain she was helping him. This boosted Kyle's confidence and he continued with renewed vigor.

"Okay, so this is your mother," he said as he eased back into the vision.

"Kyle," Simone said in a loud whisper, "get more

validating information from Alyssa's mother. Ask how she crossed over."

Kyle stared at the mother again and asked, "How did you cross over? Oh damn! I feel extremely restless here. It's very hot and now I see a wall of flames!" Kyle's breathing became shallow and his voice grew louder. He was speaking in more excited short bursts. It was as if the mother had taken over his person. The relaxed atmosphere had turned to one of fear and confusion.

"Fire – help me! I'm sorry, forgive me, I'm sorry," Kyle said.

"Okay, okay," said Simone, "let's change direction here. Alyssa, is this accurate?"

Alyssa was crying so much she couldn't answer.

Simone repeated, "Alyssa, I'm sorry dear, but I take from your reaction that this is accurate?"

"I'm sensing this was a terrible accident involving a house being destroyed by fire," Simone said. Alyssa only nodded.

"Kyle, we want to shift our focus from getting information to offering assistance to Alyssa's mother. Say to her that she is loved and what happened was an accident. Although it was a serious tragedy, she is forgiven, she is loved."

"Alyssa, what was your mother's name?" Kyle asked.

"Is – what 'is' your mother's name," Simone interjected.

"Grace," Alyssa whispered through the tears.

Kyle began again, "Grace, you are loved. We are here

to tell you, you are loved. We are sorry for your tragedy, but it was an unfortunate accident. Don't hold it against yourself.

"Oh damn," Kyle said under his breath. His low tolerance for perspiring was breached under the stress of the situation. Moisture was running freely down his face. He reached into his pocket and produced a handkerchief to wipe his forehead and face. Then Kyle thought maybe Gladys could direct Grace toward the light everyone talks about. "Grace, assistance is coming. Look for Gladys. She will show you the light. Don't be afraid."

"Okay, okay," interrupted Simone rather abruptly. "Kyle, who is Gladys?"

"Gladys is my spirit guide."

"Oh, you're more advanced than I thought. Class, give me a moment to communicate with Alyssa's mother." With that, Simone was instantly in some sort of trance, off on the mission of what the class would later learn was called spirit resolve. After a minute, she was back, focusing on the class.

"Let's ask Alyssa for verification. Alyssa dear, do you feel up to telling us?"

"It's all so true. My mother had a habit of smoking in bed. My husband and I had refused to let our daughter stay overnight with mom until she promised to never smoke in bed again. She did agree to quit smoking in bed, she promised us. Mom had given us a getaway weekend as a gift for our wedding anniversary and she would watch our daughter." Her voice trailed off as she began to cry again.

"Your mom was smoking in bed and burned down

your house and they both crossed over?"

"I swore I would never forgive her, never!" Alyssa screamed. "It was her house that burned. We had taken our daughter to her house. It's been three years. I suppose I could find it in my heart to forgive her since she seemed so upset. Simone, do you think she can hear me?"

"Why certainly. You can speak out loud or just to yourself, she'll hear you either way."

"Thank you." Alyssa was off on her own mission of forgiving her mother.

"Let's take a 10-minute break." Simone said.

Upon returning from the break, Simone suggested to Alyssa that she consider scheduling a private session with her, to try connecting with her daughter. It would be a gift from her for letting the class intrude on such a delicate part of her life. Alyssa agreed to do so.

Another woman in the class asked Simone if she had time for a question.

"Yes, that is why I'm here."

"How is it that Alyssa's mother came through but not the daughter?"

"That's because of the urgency of the woman, she overshadowed the daughter. I did sense the daughter's presence, but would really like to connect with her in a more intimate space such as in a private reading. She probably will appear to be somewhat older than when she crossed over. That is generally my finding. In spirit, we are able to be the age we desire. The spirit life is governed by our thoughts, so it seems most choose to be a median age, neither too old nor too young. Most of the time though, they will communicate their age at the time of passing to me through thought transference.

"Is she a ghost?" the woman asked. "The mother, I mean, is she a ghost?"

"As popular, and somewhat romantic, as ghost stories and legends of hauntings are," Simone explained, "they may not exist the way we traditionally thought. Today there is an array of theories about what is really happening in a classic haunting. Possibly there is no such thing as a haunting. There are some that believe the departed who crossed suddenly or tragically remain unaware that they have left the physical. They believe the deceased person is obsessed with completing a mission, so to speak, and keeps repeating the final portion of his or her life. I am not in this camp.

"There are others who believe that the physical location of a traumatic event records the event. Have you ever experienced eerie vibes in certain places? Then people who are sensitive to such unseen vibrational recordings come along and experience a subtle repeat of the recorded event. I believe this is very possible. Then too, there is the possibility of spirit people trying to communicate with physical people at the location of a tragedy simply because the ones on this side are attuned to any anomaly. This would be real-time contact, but you can see how it confuses the situation.

"Haunting, indelible vibration, real-time spirit contact, there is so much we don't know. Nevertheless, I intend to bring into the light all those I come upon who have crossed with trauma and may have some residual uneasiness. By light I mean a peaceful state of wellbeing."

As the rest of the evening continued, Kyle noted with surprise that spirit contacts seemed to be there for the asking, just waiting for someone in the physical to beckon. Alyssa went last. It was ironic that her scanning hand stopped on Kyle.

"I'm so nervous," exclaimed Alyssa as she stood before the class.

"That's understandable, you have been through a lot tonight," said Simone.

"Just relax and let it happen, then report what you see."

"I'm sorry Kyle," Alyssa apologized after a minute of silence, "all I see is a woman in white standing some distance behind you. There doesn't seem to be a message, she's just waiting. Maybe she's watching over you."

"We're really not trying to reach a conclusion to what we see," Simone said, "just to report what we see, don't analyze. The brain will make up a story as to the vision you are having, but that story is rarely accurate. We want to disengage the brain as much as we can, just like in meditation. That's fine, Alyssa, you can take your seat while we finish. I want to thank everyone for coming out tonight. Be careful driving home."

Kyle was appreciative of the opportunity to get practical experience. As he steered his car in the direction of work, he thanked Gladys for her involvement in the class.

"Gladys, two years ago I never even knew any of this was possible. Talking to the dead, who would have thought?"

Just then Kyle had the most bone-chilling feeling, he had to pull to the shoulder of the dark, deserted road he was taking as a shortcut. The feeling dissipated, but pressure was building quickly inside the top front of his head, causing the all too familiar dizzy feeling, the kind he would experience before one of his significant spiritual dreamlike events. This night's dizziness was distinct. He felt the presence of Gladys with him stronger than anytime before. There was no fear, just a deep sense of love. "Gladys, is that you? I know you're here. Is there a message? I'm listening."

"My dear Kyle, when will you believe? You have been practicing mediumship for over half your life. You have spoken to a person in spirit, to me, Gladys, and at great length. We have developed a deep, loving relationship. You had been visited that very first day by Hannah, another in spirit, and then again by her in a dream state.

Then, there was Jeane. You were with her at a critical time – her transition to eternal life. You didn't imagine these, they happened. Doubt is okay, but at some point, you have to believe. Kyle, believe!"

As he continued his way to work, he realized how elements of a life can change and have meaning when least expected and in the oddest of places. A bit paradoxical he thought, finding such clarity on such a dark untraveled road like this. He thought too that his spiritual journey was like this road, less traveled.

"Gladys, I'm sorry if I wasted time getting to this point. Thank you for never giving up on me. I'm a true believer. Now, if only Samantha would believe."

*   *   *

While the weeks passed, time frequently became a blur. During one particular week, each night Kyle would have the same intuitive message about a co-worker, Tish. The message was alarming. In the message, Tish was about to become pregnant, a normally happy occurrence, but the message told him that one parent would want the child, while the other would not. This disturbed him, since Tish was only 22 and recently engaged.

The upcoming weekend was Mother's Day. While Kyle was working with Tish, she said to him in a low voice, "Who knows, maybe next Mother's Day, I'll be a mother myself."

That's it, he said to himself, *she's pregnant.* To her he said, "That would be wonderful Tish!"

Three weeks later, Kyle noticed that Tish had stopped wearing her engagement ring to work. He delicately asked her about it, inquiring if it had been irritating her hand in the warmer weather or if she had lost it.

"I'm afraid my fiancé wants out of our relationship. I'm upset, but I'm just thankful it happened sooner, rather than later."

Then the most peculiar of things happened. Whenever Tish walked by, there was an older woman in spirit walking with her that Kyle could see.

"It's just like at Simone's class where I saw that other woman's mother," he told Samantha one evening. "This woman is saying she is Tish's grandmother and that she is aware her granddaughter is pregnant. Why is this happening, Samantha? Am I supposed to tell her something concerning her pregnancy? I don't know if that's appropriate at work."

"Kyle, you have to stop with these messages at work," she replied. "It's bordering on insanity. Certainly don't say anything, you can't jeopardize your job."

Although he did nothing, the vision of the grandmother persisted, but only at work when he was near Tish. After a few weeks, when Tish had returned from a two-week absence, the feeling of urgency with the grandmother had transposed into feelings of support and caring. Kyle would often see the grandmother with her arm around Tish's shoulder, walking side by side. She seemed to be interacting with her. It was a very tender scene for sure, but one he could not understand.

*   *   *

"Here Kyle, this came for you." Samantha handed Kyle a small brown envelope from the day's mail.

"I wonder what this is," he said, opening it up. "Hey, it's the tape of Gladys! I forgot all about this." Attached to the cassette's case was a sticky note reading: "Sorry for the delay, request was misplaced."

Kyle got his cassette recorder and began to play the tape while they prepared dinner. The man on the tape identified himself and he was indeed the author of the manual on mediumship that Kyle had received. He explained that, although he knew quite a bit about Gladys Osborne Leonard from his studies, he would endeavor to push aside his knowledge while he conducted the session. As the tape continued, Kyle listened in amazement. He was certain the person on the recording had no idea about the impact of his words.

Dinner was ready and Kyle thought the time should be spent in conversation with Samantha. He turned off the recorder. Gladys would have to wait for now. After dinner, Kyle took the tape to the office to listen further and to write a list of validating information. The soft-spoken voice on the tape began again.

"Gladys is saying what you have experienced is valid, there is a link with you. She is showing me a Ouija board and I believe that is probably how she started connecting with spirit herself."

Kyle had a bit of a different take. Since he had read online that the method Gladys and her friends used to connect with spirit was called table tipping, he knew Gladys was validating that first day of contact with him, back in college. The tape continued as he took notes.

"Don't be so critical of what you have received. Doubt is okay, for you can never be 100% certain. Some part of this though, you must accept on faith. Take the leap of faith. You are being guided very clearly. A writing instrument is being given to you. Many in spirit are aware and interested in the writing you are about to do."

Kyle stopped the tape and rewound it just a bit to replay the last part. Before he could start it again, he heard

Samantha calling.

"Coffee's ready! Kyle, coffee?"

"Yes, I would love a cup. Let's have it in the office."

He ran downstairs to give her a hand. With both of them comfortably situated in the office, he pressed the play button.

"You are being guided very clearly. A writing instrument is being given to you. Many in spirit are aware and interested in the writing you are about to do. Finally, my friend, she is smiling and coming close. She says to you: thank you for the love, thank you for the flower. She is fading now. I sincerely hope this has been helpful to you. Thank you for the opportunity. Godspeed."

"Well, that's it," Kyle said as he quickly retrieved the tape. "I'm impressed."

"Yes, it was interesting." Samantha lifted her cup as if to say cheers. He rolled his eyes intending to mock himself. He never wanted to appear too exuberant in front of Samantha.

"What did I miss while I was downstairs?" Samantha asked.

"Oh, just some peculiar likes and characteristics that Gladys and I have in common. Remember when we were in that nicer antiques store in Lambertville and I was temporarily fascinated with the teapot collection? Apparently Gladys had a collection of teapots, each one a gift from an appreciative client. Maybe she was with us, influencing me. Also her disdain for television, another idiosyncrasy we share."

"What was that last part? 'Thank you for the flower,' I

think he said."

Kyle looked confused as if he didn't understand and shrugged his shoulders. "I don't know. I'll have to listen to it again. Right now, I have to get ready for work." In reality, he knew all too well what it meant.

Samantha gathered the empty cups and returned downstairs while Kyle stayed in the office pretending to find a safe place for the tape. He thought of the reference to the flower, the one perfect rose as Samantha had called it. It had been a gesture of love from Hannah and he had given it to Gladys instead of Samantha. How was he to know the flower existed in the physical?

KYLE FINDS HIS MENTOR

Kyle soon got restless again for more training experience. It was a private type of feeling, an inner calling to keep traveling on his spiritual path. He went searching through the current month's *Creative Wisdom,* which, because of its popularity in both Pennsylvania and New Jersey, had become his sole source of available activities. He found what he was looking for. He found a class offered about 30 miles away in New Jersey, taught by a man named Stephen Westville. Kyle thought a man's perspective might be interesting, since most metaphysical classes were taught by women.

Stephen answered the phone when Kyle called to inquire about the class.

"Yes, there is an opening in the class that is beginning in two weeks," he said. "We would be delighted to have you as a participant. You can pay when you get here, all at once or a little each week. The class is eight weeks."

By the sound of his voice, Kyle assumed Stephen was from England and since he had visited the website and seen his picture, Kyle thought Stephen to be around 70.

"Follow the directions on my website," Stephen continued. "When you get to my street, just look for the house with the picket fence. We hold class in my home. What is your name again?"

"Kyle, Kyle Saint Rouse. Just call me Kyle."

"That's fine, Kyle. I'm looking forward to meeting you

week after next. Thank you for calling, good night."

"Thank you, sir. See you in two weeks. Good night."

* * *

"White picket fence, here it is," Kyle spoke aloud. The house was neatly painted, the grass trimmed to perfection. Beautiful flowers formed a border around the clean white picket fence. Kyle knew the next eight weeks of classes were meant to be. He always looked for a sign, some confirmation, that he was where he was supposed to be in the universe at a particular time. This lovely house, beautiful flowers and freshly painted fence were all the affirmation he needed. He had arrived! This was the next step on his path, no doubt about it. Kyle walked up the flower-lined path and was poised to ring the bell when something just didn't seem right.

"The address," he whispered, as he stared at the numbers in black attached to the doorframe. "I don't recall the address being 777. Certainly, I would have made a mental note of that." Kyle removed the directions to the house from his soft-sided brief case. "Oh, 7-2-2," he said, realizing he was more focused on what the Englishman had told him about looking for the picket fence. He crossed the street to the even side.

"There it is."

The address protruded from the ground on a stake driven into a patch of mud where grass had long ago given up growing.

"Hey, here's a picket fence of sorts, Gladys."

A picket fence, with traces of what once was white paint but was now flaking specks hanging on weather-beaten wood, seemed tired, weary and desperate for care.

Kyle lifted the latch and swung open the gate. The top hinge came loose and the gate collapsed, blocking the entrance. If ever there was a sign he was anticipating, this was not it.

He thought of leaving, but recalled reading in the book Gladys had written, *My Life in Two Worlds*, about an experience she had standing in front of a Spiritualist Church. Because of its shabby appearance, she was hesitant to go in, but she did anyway and found the path for which she was searching. Kyle's path too, seemed to have led him this night to a precarious intersection – the crossroads of surreal and austere.

A sign tacked to the door said "Welcome." As Kyle entered the house, he heard voices in the next room and headed in that direction. There, all eyes were on him. A more mature man stood and said, "Welcome, you must be Kyle from Bucks County. You've had a bit of a distance coming here, any problem?"

Kyle recognized the voice of the Englishman, Stephen Westville.

"No problem, the picket fence was very helpful."

"Please have a seat, we're quite informal here. I'll introduce everyone."

Kyle sat next to the last woman introduced, Rose, who was Stephen's wife. There was a very comforting feeling about her. He was glad he had chosen the open seat next to her. She seemed to sense his apprehensiveness and whispered to him, "Everything is going to work out fine. You're at the right place."

"Let's begin." Stephen turned off the meditative music that had been playing.

"Tonight we will begin our eight-week journey together. It will be a voyage you can take as far as you wish; the key is practice. Practice what, you may ask. That's where I come in. Everything begins with awareness. How do you know about anything unless you first become aware? Through the weeks, we will move from awareness, to doing more and being more, preparing better for life and what's beyond this physical life."

The ages of the people in the class seemed to represent every decade from 20 to 70. Kyle felt comfortable and right at home, enough to send a mental message: *Gladys, thanks for leading me here.*

The weeks progressed and so did Kyle. The course was designed as a series of hands-on workshops. The classes touched on an array of topics, including aura reading, clairvoyant ability (visions from within) and clairaudient messages (hearing a voice from within but the words come from someone else by way of telepathy). Other topics included psychometry, which is the ability to "read" an object's history, and dowsing, traditionally the art of finding hidden water, minerals or other valued objects hidden underground and currently also used to find missing persons. Everything taught was intended to awaken the sixth sense and bring it closer to its full potential.

Stephen had mentioned in passing that sometimes a bump to the head, particularly in the back, could jump start the functioning of the pineal gland seated deep within the brain. This is considered to be the organ of higher vision, the link that connects the physical and spiritual worlds. Of course, he didn't recommend thumping your children on the head. You could achieve the same, in time, through meditation. Kyle thought back to the overzealous slap to his head in 2nd grade and wondered if perhaps it had provided him with a shortcut of sorts.

Stephen provided a safe place for Kyle to explore all of these long hidden abilities and to validate their use. Kyle even noticed that his card reading benefited with more confident and telling readings, and he was more willing to take risks. His clients liked that.

At the last class, Stephen said he would be conducting a guided meditation.

"Tonight, we hope to meet our spirit guide or guides, whichever the case may be. Maybe you'll meet what some consider your higher self, others say inner self, but we'll ask for our principal spirit guide and see who shows up."

Hey Gladys, Kyle said, using thought transference, *I'm going to meet you in person.*

"Let's take a short time out and everyone use the restroom, if you must," Stephen said. "As always, turn off your cell phone please."

With that, Stephen started the calming music in

preparation. Everyone soon returned to their seats and settled in.

"Looks like everyone's here, let's start. Close your eyes and just listen," he paused. "Take a deep breath through your nose and exhale completely through your mouth as if you're trying to keep a feather afloat with your breath. Good, now again."

The meditation drifted along to the point of meeting the spirit guide. Kyle wondered if Gladys would appear younger, as he had seen her online, or more the age when she crossed over. Would she be wearing clothes from her day?

"The door opens now and out walks someone toward you saying, 'It's good to see you, welcome,'" continued Stephen. "Now spend the next several minutes together and mentally ask questions, like the person's name. You may want to verify that you are on the correct path, or simply enjoy each other's company in silence."

Kyle relaxed as much as he could. He was cautious about getting too excited. He remembered that a sudden spike in one's excitement level would probably end the vision. Better to approach spirit communication with enthusiasm, but not over-the-top elation.

The door was opening. Out came a figure walking toward him.

"Marcel?"

Kyle initially observed Marcel toward the end of his first marriage. Kyle had been practicing therapeutic massage on disabled children and young adults and on older stroke patients, trying to find some purpose in his life. As he worked on his clients, he would spontaneously see Marcel, in spirit, standing at various places around the massage table. At times, Marcel would point out the origin or real cause of the client's pain. Because of this, Kyle originally thought him to be a healing guide. Of course, he didn't know Marcel's name or if the vision was real or imaginary. That information was revealed much later, after Kyle had started his meditation routine, long after Kyle had accepted the idea of Gladys being his primary spirit guide. Until Kyle's discovery, in 1999, of Gladys' year of passing, he assumed she had been with him from birth. After that, he had never given thought to his first two decades of life in the physical. In error, he continued to think of Gladys as his primary guide since he had been aware of her longer and she had a more pronounced presence in his life.

In Kyle's visions, Marcel is as tall as Kyle, good looking with bronze skin and perfectly silver hair. He wears a violet robe with an upright gray collar that has a swirl-type design woven into the fabric.

"It is my purpose to bring you closer to the truth," Marcel began. "The life before this, you could not hear clearly, though we were together as now.

"There is a plane of existence outside of the physical plane, it is the spiritual realm, a place of absolute love and truth. The origin of each soul, the spirit eternal, exists permanently in this realm. You are never without a presence in this spiritual dwelling. It is here that the story of one's life in the physical is inspired and created. This is a life plan and is decided upon in the fairest of manners by the one who is to put on the cloak of the physical. Others, whose life plans intertwine, do likewise. This is an ongoing process and is assisted closely by the spiritual hierarchy.

"Wait, didn't God plan my life?" Kyle asked.

"We must accept responsibility for our own life plan," Marcel answered.

"The soul is guided, while in the physical, through intuition. Yet, some life plan decisions are difficult to participate in and give rise to fear. This creates disharmony within and guidance seems distant and unclear. The feeling of abandonment becomes pervasive, but losing faith in one's life plan and ending your life in the physical is not a solution. An act of despair is a decision never made in the spirit realm.

"What about dying? Certainly God chooses my time for passing."

"This is God's plan: that all decisions concerning you, even the time of your transition, are made by you. This is the fairest manner. When one realizes that whatever takes place in their physical life, they had a hand in planning, fear of the future and despair can be eliminated."

"Can a decision made in the spiritual realm ever be changed?"

"Yes, decisions are changed, but limitations do exist. With others involved in your life plan, at some juncture it can no longer be altered. This is the feeling you refer to as 'etched in stone' when you are assisting those who call on you for guidance."

"Me, offering guidance?"

"You are being assisted closely. The readings, as you call them, they are encouragement and guidance. You have a sensitivity to read the life plan of others. At times, there is confusion when someone is about to ask for a change."

"Why are there negative situations, such hardships in some lives?" Kyle asked.

"We must always remember, we are but a small part of a broader vision. The spiritual evolution of humankind is dependent on cooperation. Negativity, as you say, is the preferred, uncomplicated way to initiate the idea of cooperation or provide an opportunity to right injustice. In reality, negativity does not exist, just opportunities, neither good nor bad.

"There was a time just before this life, as I mentioned, you could not hear me clearly. You worked on a railroad in Poland shoveling coal to feed the locomotive. It was among the lowest of times on the earth plane. You unknowingly transported many to their last days in the physical. You believed the false story yourself and were slow to explore the uneasy feeling within. When you discovered the horrors, you denied outwardly that such atrocities were happening, but inwardly you knew. The faster your hunched figure shoveled in disgrace, it seemed the faster the train traveled to the death camps. Your back ached, your spirit was broken. You became dead inside.

"Finally, you were unable to continue. You ended your life in the physical. It was 1942 and you were 22. You left behind an intended bride who continued on but never recovered from your leaving. She suffered greatly through the war and after, working tirelessly, in your memory, to right the wrongs. She succumbed to life itself the year before you were born into this physical body. Her birth followed the next year. You met her again in this life and agreed to unite. However, she could not release the deep hurt she harbored from the past. You both agreed to a change.

"Your crooked spine was your request to symbolize the weight of the guilt you carried from that former life, to always remember there are differences and to set you free from the shame.

"While in spirit, you asked for an opportunity to amend for your act of hopelessness, to help others in despair. The spiritual encounters you are experiencing, the support and guidance you are getting and sharing, are because you asked.

"This is a new day. You can help heal the troubled hearts. You can bring hope to those in despair. It's really love everyone is searching for, self-acceptance and reciprocal love. Eventually love can extend throughout the community and beyond. Love has no boundaries."

"Where do I start?" Kyle asked.

"In the mirror," Marcel laughed. "We all start by looking at our self and accepting the one within. Kyle, you've already started. Now, you must lead others to learn to love themselves. You must tell them that the support and encouragement they need is on our side – the side of spirit – but, one must ask for help before we are permitted to assist. It is here waiting. We are here, a breath away. Tell them, you are being guided."

Then Marcel and the vision faded as Stephen's voice brought the class back to consciousness.

URGENCY

Kyle enrolled in Stephen's very next class. Four months had passed since the first series of classes and it was good to get back to that little dilapidated house with the big feeling of warmth and welcome inside.

As he entered the house, Kyle sensed something unusual. It was a feeling to hurry, before it's too late. With the introduction of each class member and Stephen outlining the direction in which he would lead this class, the feeling was soon overshadowed by the work at hand. However, after class, as Kyle traveled to his job, the feeling resurfaced. He had time to sort it out. It felt as if someone were dying.

In the morning, when he returned home, Kyle sent Stephen an email with the feeling of serious illness but never mentioning the word death in the message. Stephen replied that he wasn't feeling well the evening before. He had been to the dentist earlier in the day and had extensive work done. To make matters worse, he was trying to shed a few pounds and that never is a pleasant experience. In short, if Kyle was picking up health issues about someone, it probably was him.

"More experience is what I need," Kyle was telling Samantha at dinner that evening.

"Kyle, you're getting plenty of experience, be patient. Maybe you're worrying about the psychic party that's coming up.

"Yes, I was just thinking of the party. I ran into my

former co-worker Lisa and she said how much everyone is looking forward to it. I am too, but I do feel pressure. I don't want to disappoint."

"The party's not for another month. You say you're good at this, why don't you just relax and have fun?"

Finally it was Thursday, the day before the psychic party at Lisa's house. Kyle was required to work overtime and arrived home later than he had planned with a feeling of dizziness in his head. He was aware another message was most likely coming through. Although he was always curious and appreciative of any message he would receive, he just didn't have time to meditate right then. He hurried to pack the items he needed for the party. If something was missing, he would have time to buy it.

Whereas Samantha considered Kyle's work hours a detriment to his so-called psychic ability, Kyle thought somehow his work hours helped. The constant rushing around and somewhat regular sleep deprivation meant that Kyle never had a chance to focus on any mental anxiety that might detract from his psychic skill.

It was 1 p.m. Kyle went to bed, laid his head on the pillow and again became aware of the dizziness.

"Kyle."

A child's voice was calling his name. He was in a room with no windows or doors. In the center of the room, a ball of light was quickly developing into a young girl who Kyle thought to be about 9. She had long blonde hair and was wearing a soft white gown.

"Kyle," she said again in a gentle tone. "I have had many incarnations on the earth plane. I have danced the rituals at Stonehenge, explored the seas of the Old World and seen my own demise as an indigenous person on the plains of your country. I have the empathy, passion and wisdom of each experience within me. I am here with you as a young girl, to represent innocence and tell you that all spirit beings have already been created and cannot be destroyed. Humankind cannot prevent a soul from entering the physical plane. Guilt is not from the will of the Creator but rather the mind of man. A lifetime of guilt is too severe. Soon, this shall have meaning."

With that, she was gone.

Kyle slept until Samantha woke him for dinner. He didn't plan it that way, but had forgotten to set the alarm. At dinner he tried to relate the girl and the dream to Samantha in a meaningful way, but couldn't. Although he did recall her saying that soon this would have meaning.

On Friday morning, when he arrived home from work, the house was quiet and he had no trouble falling asleep, resting his body for the party. Soon it was time to leave.

"Good luck Kyle! Remember, have fun," Samantha said as she kissed him goodbye.

He drove off and pushed a Josh Groban CD into the car's player to calm the nervousness in his abdomen. He had no idea who Lisa had invited to the party. He never asked her if there would be someone he knew. Since they worked at the same place, he never wanted to give the impression that he was researching a person before reading them.

"Hey everyone, the psychic has arrived!" Lisa announced when Kyle entered the house. "This is my co-worker, Kyle." She introduced him to the five other women.

"Very nice to meet everyone." He turned to Lisa and asked for her help with the rest of the things in his car.

"Tish from work is bringing two other people and should be coming any minute," Lisa said. "She's a bit nervous about her reading, since she works with you and may decide not to have one herself, but she did promise to bring the others."

Just then, Tish and the others drove up. Kyle managed an awkward wave with his arms full of the remaining items. He returned to the house ahead of Lisa, while she waited to escort the last three guests inside.

Kyle went down the stairs to the basement where he would be reading. He set up the table, chairs and recorder and began the routine that always preceded readings. He practiced deep breathing and recited aloud his mantra, a group of syllables that caused a subtle vibration in his head, transporting him to a slightly altered state of consciousness. Then he asked for assistance from those he called his spirit support group.

There was Grandmom Maria. After the demonstration of mediumship with Simone, Kyle accepted the fact that his maternal grandmother was around him frequently. He acknowledged his grandmother's presence and asked her to assist during his readings. Next there was Adele, who came to Kyle through Larry, a classmate from Stephen's first session of classes. Larry was one of the better mediums in the class who had enrolled for an opportunity to practice.

As Kyle sat for Larry to give him a reading, Larry called out the name of Kyle's first mother-in-law saying, "Adele is with you. She says it is great to finally be able to hear you. Thanks for remembering me." As simple as the message was, it held a powerful meaning for Kyle. He was very fond of Adele and although his marriage ended in turmoil, he thought of her as a fair and loving woman. While she was in the physical, Adele had a serious, uncorrectable hearing problem. When Kyle would speak to her, since his voice was of a softer nature even when he tried to shout, she just couldn't hear him very well. Now in spirit, she could hear him. Kyle had asked her also if she would sit during his readings and add her support to the group. He felt she had accepted.

Then there was Peter, a man five years younger than Kyle. They had worked together occasionally and for some unknown reason, Kyle could see Peter's future very clearly. He saw that Peter was about to discover he had a terminal illness and would cross over very quickly, within a year.

Occasionally in conversation, Peter would touch on a topic of a metaphysical nature, almost as if testing Kyle's reaction. Kyle took this as permission to pursue the topic and Peter's eyes grew big like saucers when Kyle described a man in spirit standing next to Peter at work one night.

"Constantine!" Kyle shouted. "Something like that with a hard 'C' that sounds like a 'K.' He is emphatic that it is spelled with a C."

"Very good," laughed Peter. "That is my Ukrainian

uncle, the man that raised me when my father died. When they moved to this country, his name was Americanized from a K to a C with a few additional letter changes. He was very self-conscious about his name. So, you see him with me?"

"I do. He is saying something to the effect that our old habits seem to catch up with us. I am seeing him now, smoking a cigarette."

"Oh, that's him telling me I smoke too much. You should have seen him smoke. I'm surprised he got any sleep," Peter said with a broad smile.

"Did he pass from lung cancer?" Kyle asked. "I'm feeling quite a bit of chest pressure."

"No, he died in a car accident, but there may have been considerable chest pressure from the way the car looked after the accident."

Shortly after that night, Peter was missing from work with a malaise, or so he thought. After testing, it was discovered he had stage-four cancer. Peter crossed over eight months from the time Kyle had seen his uncle.

Three months later, Peter's wife had called Kyle to schedule an appointment. She explained that although he didn't know her, Peter had spoken very highly of him. Now she was calling to reach out to Peter through Kyle.

Her appointment came and as they sat in Kyle's house, Peter indeed did appear next to her for Kyle to see. He spoke about things that only his wife would know. He mentioned the jewelry he had bought for her upcoming birthday just before he was unable to get around and how it went hidden and forgotten in the old secretary desk. He mentioned how his wife did find it and where she was sitting while she opened the gift. He showed Kyle an image of a gold bracelet of interlocking hearts. This was the gift, the last symbol of love for his wife. He described how she sat frozen in that chair for an hour, crying every last tear. He left her with the message that their love wasn't dead, but stronger than ever. He was with her now and always would be while she needed him.

After that reading, Kyle asked Peter to join his support group to sit with the others during his readings. He felt Peter enthusiastically obliged. Of course there was Gladys, Jeane Dixon, and Marcel. There in the basement, Kyle petitioned in prayer his invisible support group. Then he felt ready for the first client of the evening and went upstairs.

"Before I begin," he started as he faced the group, "I want to assure all of you that I will not remember anything I tell you this evening, so if I know you or we should meet again, there is no reason to feel awkward. I am now ready for the first guest. Just come downstairs when you're ready."

Kyle returned to the basement, took his seat, mentally focused on his support group and placed a cassette into the recorder. He heard footsteps on the stairs. Since the staircase was enclosed, it wasn't until the very last step that he saw Tish.

"Hi Tish, thank you for this opportunity."

"Are you sure you won't remember what you tell me?"

"Absolutely. You see, I'm in some type of trance or altered state of consciousness. I won't remember a thing."

"Great, let's start," she said as she took her seat.

"Don't tell me anything bad."

Kyle laughed. "That is my Number One request, nothing bad. I don't believe in bad. We seem to assign good or bad to every situation, but I do know what you mean, so don't worry, nothing bad."

Kyle began by picking the Queen of Clubs from the deck of cards he was holding. Lifting it up slightly, he mentally said – *This card will represent Tish*. He had determined her to be that card because of her gender and hair color, dark brown. He then randomly placed the card back in the deck and began to shuffle until it felt right to stop. He placed the cards on the table face up, one at a time, in groups of eight. When he had done this three times, he discarded the remainder of the deck and went noticeably silent.

"Now Tish," he began, "if I see a deceased person around you, would you want me to speak about this?"

"Yes," was her quick reply.

"There is a woman in spirit next to you, on your left." Suddenly he realized this was the same woman he had seen with Tish at work, her grandmother. He felt a tremendous feeling of peace and continued.

"Tish, there is a woman presenting herself as your grandmother. Don't say anything just yet. Let me validate this first. She was about 5'5" when she was on our side. She crossed over at approximately age 76 from...umm...I'm mentally asking her how she passed. She's not real clear here, so I'll say she was in a coma when she passed but it was precipitated by...I'm seeing a grey cloudy area in her chest –

pneumonia?"

"That's good, Kyle, can I talk now?"

"Sure."

"That is my Grams. She was 5'5" and passed away one week before her 76th birthday. She was in a coma at her passing from complications of her diabetes, but she did have pneumonia. Is she really here? She died 11 years ago. Maybe you're just picking up my memory of her."

"I know, from doing this so often," Kyle said, "that there is something timely to a visit from our loved ones in spirit as opposed to a memory. It has been my experience that they seem to be acutely aware of what we are doing, which would eliminate the idea of being a memory."

"Well, how did you get her here?"

"I can't take credit for your Grams being here, just for seeing her. It's my belief that many in spirit are around us much of the time. I've come to believe we share the same space. Everyone knows the paradigm of heaven and hell, but maybe it's different. Perhaps those final resting places come much later in time, if at all. I'm not too keen on the idea of hell."

"Okay, so why is she here, Kyle?"

"I get the sense that she is here, and has been with you for quite some time, to comfort you. She is stroking the side of your head now and leans closer and is kissing your head. Of course there is a tremendous feeling of love here. I know that sounds so generic, but I feel a strong pull, like a magnetic attraction between the two of you.

She is turning to me and saying the dream, tell the dream."

"What dream?" Tish asked.

Kyle thought for a moment. He intuitively knew her grandmother was referring to the dream of the previous day in which the young girl appeared. How did she know about his dream? Kyle felt his head begin to get dizzier and he knew a message of great importance was here to be exchanged from the world of spirit to the world of the physical and he was the messenger. He took a deep relaxing breath, slowly exhaled and felt himself go deeper into the trance state.

"Tish, I see next to you," he pointed to her right side, "a ball of light. I've seen this before around some women. I call it a ball of energy. It is my symbol for the idea of an unborn child. I want to be very clear here, this ball of energy or light is just a symbol to me, so I would know to talk about an unborn child. It is not an actual unborn child. Again, there is no unborn child really there, just a symbol. Do you understand?"

"Yes," she said as tears began rolling down her cheeks.

Kyle recalled the time from work when he received the message: *One would want the child, the other not.* Now, it was validated and the dream from the day before made sense, too. Kyle was reluctant to begin, but sensed his own support group moving closer behind him, as if to lend their encouragement to continue.

"Tish, the dream your grandmother referred to is one I had just yesterday. I didn't understand it then, but now it seems to have meaning. In the dream, a young girl appeared and said that all spirit beings have already been created. She said that no one could prevent a soul from ultimately entering the physical world. I interpreted this as meaning being born and I feel she meant that another plan for that soul to enter the physical world would be put into action. She said guilt is from the minds of men, not the will of God. Yes, I recall very clearly: she said 'A lifetime of guilt is too severe.' I hope this brings some resolution to you. It is not important for me to know your personal story, I'm just passing this message to you."

"Yes, Kyle it has meaning," Tish said through the tears, breaking down even further. "I had to make a very emotional decision not too long ago. I wanted that baby Kyle, I did – I really did, but I couldn't bring a child into the world as a single mother. My parents frowned upon that. What would our relatives think? What would their friends think? What would their church congregation think? My whole decision revolved around other people's opinions. I never seemed to matter! The baby never mattered! After a while, I was so weary. Today, I regret the decision I made." She went silent, sobbing into a handful of tissues.

"Now your grandmother stands beside you to support you and the rationale or understanding of your decision. She nods her head once to me and is saying, 'Thank you.' She is fading from my sight now, but I still feel her presence. Be aware that she is around you and acknowledge her presence by talking to her mentally. Or, you can speak aloud, it doesn't matter. Ask her for support and encouragement."

Kyle redirected his attention to the card groupings on the table and after a few moments of quiet for Tish to compose herself, he continued.

"Hey, Tish, looks like true love is just around the corner. I see here a tall, light-haired male coming your way. He seems to be reading many books in this vision and he seems to be connected to a university in some way."

"That's Bill," she said excitedly, "I already met him and yes, he is connected with a university; he's an associate professor. He also does some research for his brother's consulting firm. What do the cards say? Does this relationship look good?"

"It looks perfect and will be heading into a more serious phase in about two months. You may even move in together, but will eventually get married and from what I see, you will have two children. Congratulations!"

"Thanks! I'll take this future gladly!" Just then the timer rang.

"Oh no," Kyle said, "that 20 minutes went awfully fast. I didn't get to tell you that much. I'm sorry we spent so much time…"

"No Kyle, don't you see," Tish said, "it was meant to be this way? To think, I wasn't going to get a reading, but I had a dream last night myself. It was Grams in the dream and we were driving to see you. Thanks Kyle, you really have eased my mind and my heart."

They both stood. Tish leaned across the narrow table

and kissed Kyle on the cheek.

"Oh thanks, Tish. Thanks too for having an open mind about this. Please send the next person down."

As she disappeared up the stairs, Kyle reflected on the last few minutes. He could see there was purpose to it all. He expressed his gratitude to those with him in spirit. He wondered how Tish's grandmother knew about his dream.

More footsteps on the stairs and another guest appeared. Kyle was surprised to see a middle aged man this time.

"The name's Sylvester," he said as he extended his hand, "my old man had a sense of humor, Sylvester Palmieri. My friends call me Lights-Out. You can call me Al, my middle name."

"Al - Whew! That's some grip you have. Nice to meet you. Have a seat."

"Nice meetin' you too."

"I'm sorry, Al, I didn't see you upstairs when I was about to start."

"Oh, I'm Lisa's uncle. I was in the area and stopped in to visit my sister, Lisa's mother, who lives across the street. She was coming here so I thought I'd catch a visit with my goddaughter Lisa too. Lisa said someone had to leave and asked if I could take their place so there'd be enough people. Are you really as good as they were talkin' about upstairs?"

"I suppose we're going to find out."

Kyle was trying to be convincing but he was put off by Al's somewhat brash demeanor. Kyle sensed a signal of discord coming from him. Al was relatively short, 5'6" at best, but he was massive in width and weight. Although he wore a black T-shirt, he was impeccably dressed in what Kyle thought was an Armani suit, having glanced at the label when Al opened the jacket to retrieve a cigar.

"Don't worry, I won't be lightin' up. I'm curious to know what you see."

"I'm curious too, Al. Let's start."

Kyle searched the deck for the King of Clubs to represent this dark-haired man. As he shuffled the deck, Kyle began having a vision. He saw a room full of beautiful flowers and what appeared to be three wooden boxes. When he focused on the boxes, they appeared to be caskets. He thought he had gotten the message.

"Al, you're a funeral director?"

Al burst out in laughter.

"No, not a funeral director, but I guess you can say I'm connected with the industry."

"It's just that I'm seeing so many flowers, especially orchids."

"That's good. Orchids are my passion. I have a green house on my property, grow lots of beautiful flowers. Few people know that about me though."

Kyle felt uneasy to mention the caskets and thought it better to wait. Another vision was forming. In this image, Al was standing with another man at a construction site. Two ideas were being impressed at the same time: that it was a commercial site and that it was in New Jersey. Initially, it appeared the men were shaking hands but a few seconds into the visualization, he sensed that Al was intimidating the other man to see things his way. Kyle felt uneasy with the length of silence. He wasn't sure if the uneasiness was from him or if he was picking it up from Al. He hastened to talk again.

"Al, you conduct business in New Jersey? I am getting the idea that you have short assignments, scattered about in Jersey and you work on the fringe of a bigger organization, making sure that everything is flowing correctly. Is this making sense?"

"Yeah, that makes perfect sense, Kyle. You could say I'm a project management consultant. I help people get things done in Jersey: commercial projects, casinos, union contracts. Like you said, short assignments. Very good! What else you see?"

Just then, Kyle's abdomen began to tighten. It seemed to be some kind of warning. Another vision was forming in which Kyle clearly saw Al pushing three men, one at a time, off the edge of something resembling a quarry. The apprehension within Kyle was building. This triggered Kyle's perspiration response and sweat began rolling down his face.

"Gettin' hot, eh? What else you see?" questioned Al.

Kyle always wanted to be accurate; it was his weakness. The last remnants of his ego, perhaps, but his reputation also depended on it. He felt a true dedication to the craft of reading someone's life plan. However, should there be retribution for knowing too much, he had others in his life to consider. Just then, a man very much resembling Marcel walked directly into the vision, but appeared to be in the forefront. Kyle determined he was not part of the vision, but bringing a separate message altogether. The man faced forward.

"Kyle, you must stop! You are in danger. Stop the reading."

Kyle immediately ended the vision and spoke quickly but calmly to Al.

"Al, you missed earlier in the evening when I said I wouldn't remember anything about any of the readings I did tonight, or ever, for that matter. I'm sorry, I just don't see anything else. Oh, this doesn't mean something's going to happen to you, it just means I'm a little off my game tonight in reading you. I just can't read you. Sorry, it happens every now and then."

"I understand Kyle. I thought you were doin' pretty good for a while there. Well, no sense in takin' time away from someone else."

Al stood and shook Kyle's hand again with his pit-bull grip.

"I like you. Next time we meet, I'll tell you how I got the name Lights-Out."

"Al, it was a pleasure, good night."

Al ascended the stairs and Kyle thought the room shook with each step until he realized it was his nerve-racked body returning to normal. He hoped he had persuaded Al to believe him, but before he could convince himself he was safe, someone else in spirit was tugging on him for his attention.

He said his name was Paul and he was there with a

warning for the next person. Kyle sensed he was extremely agitated but felt he was not a threat, although Kyle didn't believe in threats from spirit. Just then a woman came down the last step.

"Good evening," he said. "I'm Kyle. You are?" Kyle greeted her without letting on what had just transpired.

"Riley."

This woman was young, 22. She had a striking combination of beautiful blue eyes and dark hair. Kyle shuffled and dealt the cards as in the previous readings.

"Riley, if I sense a deceased person around you, would you want me to speak about that?"

"Yes, please do."

"Let's begin then. Someone named Paul is here. He is a contemporary of yours, you know, approximately your age. I believe, when he was on this side, you had a relationship with him, a romance." Kyle spoke with great speed, which he attributed to the anxiousness of Paul, the one in spirit.

"Paul was my high school boyfriend." Riley began crying.

"Please, no more!" Kyle held his right hand up to silence her. "He is screaming, ALCOHOL, ALCOHOL. Did he pass away in an alcohol-related accident?"

Riley nodded through the tears.

"I'm sorry," Kyle said, all the while thinking she was too young to handle this.

The reading went on and every aspect of her life in the upcoming year was touched upon. Her plan, as Kyle saw it, included returning to school for a graduate degree, a new relationship, of which Paul approved, a promotion at work and moving. Then it was time for her to ask questions. She had only one.

"For the last two months I attended the Alcoholics Anonymous program. I was out last weekend with my friends and had two drinks. I really think I can handle it. Does my future look like I will be able to drink?"

Kyle was taken aback temporarily.

"Dear, don't you see the big picture? Paul came here tonight to be with you, warning you of just how dangerously you are living. His shouting alcohol wasn't about his accident – it was a warning to you. It is beautiful that even though Paul is deceased, he is aware of what's going on in your life and cares enough about you. Please honor his love for you and listen. You have a lot to live for. I know you can't see it now, but it's true, you have real possibilities for a beautiful life ahead. If you can't do it for yourself, do it for Paul."

Through all the tears, she agreed to listen. Kyle thought Paul had settled down. The message was delivered. Riley dried her eyes and stood. She thanked Kyle for being so thorough.

"There is one more thing, Riley."

"What's that?"

"Paul just said that he would be leaving now. He's not afraid for you anymore."

She kissed Kyle on the cheek, reached for one last tissue and was gone.

More footsteps on the stairs, and Kyle conducted

another reading. This continued until everyone was read. Kyle packed and thanked Lisa for hosting the evening. Now it was off to work and his day would be done.

*   *   *

It was Saturday morning. Before Kyle went to bed for his three hour nap, he promised to take Samantha out for dinner and tell her how the dream made sense after all. When the time came, however, he couldn't remember the details, only that the dream made sense to someone at the party, but he couldn't remember to whom.

Stephen's class ended. It was a very productive series of sessions in which Kyle got the practice he was looking for. Shortly after, he received an email from a class member that Rose, Stephen's wife, had passed away unexpectedly.

"It was the urgency, that message about a serious illness," Kyle said to Samantha at dinner. "The message was for Rose, not Stephen."

"A room full of psychics, you would think someone could have warned her," Samantha jested.

"I know, it's kind of embarrassing."

SAMANTHA BECOMES A BELIEVER

He said his name was Nick, Samantha's cousin from Oregon, but on the phone, Kyle just couldn't place him.

"I'm Lena's son, Samantha's Aunt Lena. I don't travel east that often, I'm a bit of a recluse since the war. I don't think we ever met."

Then Kyle recalled seeing a photo on the piano at Aunt Lena's house, the soldier no one talked about.

"I'd like to see Samantha and you, if you can make time that is."

"Sure," Kyle insisted. "Samantha's not here right now, but I am certain Saturday at 5 will be perfect. We'll have dinner together here."

"Sounds good, I'll bring wine. One more thing, I heard you do some kind of intuitive readings. Is that right?"

"Yes, I do."

"Could you fit me in sometime while I'm in the area?"

"Certainly, why don't you come earlier Saturday, say 4 o'clock? We'll do a reading before dinner. It will be a gift from me."

"Well, thank you, Kyle. I'll see you then."

When Samantha came home, Kyle told her that her cousin Nick would be visiting for dinner Saturday. He thought he noticed a slight pause and some uneasiness.

"I hope you don't mind I invited him for dinner. I got the feeling he is reaching out. How come we never see him?"

"Because he's only traveled home once in 40 years, and that was for his father's funeral. He never was the same after Vietnam, moved to Oregon and poof – he disappeared."

"He did ask for a reading, which we're going to do before dinner."

"A lot of good that'll do. He's been alone far too long for anything to help."

"Samantha, it's what I do. Maybe it will help or at least encourage him to see a professional for help. It might not be too late."

On Saturday, Samantha and Kyle greeted Nick at the door.

"Come in stranger, nice to see you again," Samantha said as she kissed Nick. "This is my husband, Kyle."

"Pleased to meet you, Kyle."

"Likewise! I'm sure there's plenty of catching up to do, but Nick, how 'bout we do that reading right now in the study behind you?"

"Sure, I really don't know what to expect, but my mom suggested I talk with you. Her neighbor, Tish, was at a party you were doing, said you were real good at this."

"Thanks for the vote of confidence. Small world isn't it?" They both took a seat in the study. "It's funny, you said you didn't know what to expect. I never know what to expect before each reading either. When I pray, I ask for the most beneficial information for the client to come forward. Now, let's begin."

Kyle shuffled and laid the cards out in the appropriate

fashion. As he did, he could sense a massive amount of anxiety and confusion coming from the spirit side. Silently, Kyle asked for clarity. He began having a vision of heavy smoke rolling by. Through the smoke, Kyle could see smoldering military vehicles. His attention was drawn to the fact that it was nighttime. When he realized that the idea imparted was about an attack at night on what he thought was a sleeping area, the vision cleared, except for the smoke. A man dressed in a military uniform walked forward from within the smoke.

"The name is Ernie, Lieutenant Ernie, soldier. Keep alert. I got a bad feeling. You got the letter?"

"Did you know an Ernie during the war? There's a Lieutenant Ernie here; he's mentioning something about a letter."

"I'm sorry Ernie. It was a mistake – I swear!" Nick shouted as he began to cry.

"Whoa boy! Soldiers don't make mistakes. At least they don't admit to them," Ernie continued. *"Any accidents or fatalities, blame it on the enemy – makes the paperwork less complicated."* Kyle did not communicate this verbatim to Nick.

"What is it about Ernie? If a situation arises, Ernie seems to be focusing on denying responsibility."

"Yes, that was the Lieutenant's style," Nick said, still shouting, "deny anything was wrong. It was a war for Christ's sake, everything was wrong! We were on our way from company headquarters to the frontline. It was a transfer for the lieutenant after coming back from medical leave and I was his driver. The last group under his command was wiped out.

Rumor had it he was being discharged but he was determined to continue his career. His Pop pulled some political strings. I suppose the only way to stay in was to go back to the front and Ernie was out to prove something.

"We had just caught up with his new platoon, who were already on the move without us because of a delay we experienced. It was becoming dark when we realized the mapping coordinates were wrong. Communications were down at battalion headquarters, so we decided to look for an area to spend the night. To our surprise, there was a clearing large enough for our platoon just beyond an area of dense jungle. I told Ernie I thought it was a setup for an ambush. It was too good to be true, but Ernie wouldn't listen. He had a reputation for exposing his men to high-risk circumstances.

"I could see he was scared and clueless. Our survival depended on Ernie's decisions and I was the one closest to him. There was talk of me popping him. A few of the men said they had heard stories of that happening in battle."

"Stop your goddamn quibbling, soldier, I'm in charge. We're spending the night here. Everything will be sorted out by morning," insisted a confused-looking Ernie in the vision.

"We pitched a tent for the lieutenant in the center of where our vehicles were secured for the night. The rest of the men took cover in the surrounding brush. I was on guard in the Jeep outside the tent. Lieutenant Ernie came out in the middle of the night and whispered to me, 'Here's a letter to my wife, just in case something goes wrong. Keep alert, I got a bad feeling.'"

"No sooner did he return to the tent, we came under attack. We were surrounded on three sides. Our vehicles were under fire first. I ran toward the tent and could hear what sounded like the lieutenant crying. I called for him to follow me and I ran for cover with the others.

"You have to understand Kyle, the confusion of battle, especially an ambush at night. Apparently, Ernie did come out and was running toward us yelling 'Hold your positions,' but we had been taking fire from every which way. The smoke from the burning vehicles was keeping visibility to a minimum – I shot Ernie. I didn't intend to, it was an accident. Nobody much cared about what happened. With Ernie out of the way, we were free to make a more reasonable decision. We hightailed it out of there. Oh, we took Ernie with us, but he was a goner. We only lost two men that night, besides Ernie. Had we stayed as ordered, well, let's just say you and I wouldn't be having this discussion."

"I'm sorry you had to go through all of this, Nick, I truly am," Kyle said. "Just curious, what happened to the letter to his wife?"

"I'm afraid I still have that letter. I kept it through the years. I could never face the wife of the man I killed. The guilt is unbearable. I still have nightmares of that day. They always end the same, until recently that is. About a month ago, I had a different dream of that day. When I was carrying the lieutenant out of there, he seemed to come alive again and said to me, 'Soldier, it's time to deliver the letter.' That's why I came east. I brought the letter with me. His wife still lives in the same house, not that far from here.

Kyle had an urge to cry and knew the man in spirit, Ernie, was closer than ever. Kyle returned his attention to the vision. He saw the burning vehicles again. This time, Ernie emerged from amidst the smoke wearing a beautiful gray suit seemingly unscathed by the event. He had his uniform draped over his shoulder.

"There's no guilt required soldier, it's just the way of war."

In one fluid movement, he swirled the uniform from his shoulder into the fire. He turned to face where Nick was seated, snapped to attention, saluted and said, *"Give Donna my love,"* then he vanished. Kyle did report this verbatim to Nick.

"Is her name Donna?"

"Yes! Yes, it is."

"Nick, I never expected this reading to unfold this way. I would say you really have to connect with Donna."

"I've been by myself for 40 years, reliving this drama, feeling the guilt. I never talked about this."

"Dinner in five minutes guys," Samantha called from the foyer.

"Kyle, I feel so relieved, you don't have to tell me another thing."

"Oh, but I will. I see you moving within three months, quite some distance too and involved in a romance before that. That could be why you're moving. The romance intensifies around six months from now. In short, you're dropping everything on the West Coast to come east."

"That's enough good news for one day. Thanks Kyle."

"Thank you for the opportunity, Nick."

"Hey, did Sam ever tell you how close we were growing up? Just like brother and sister."

The evening progressed, but it wasn't until three months later that Samantha started to value the reading Kyle had done. Nick had called to tell Kyle and Samantha that he had spent some time with Ernie's former spouse and they decided to embark on a serious relationship.

"Aunt Lena called today, Kyle, and said she thought she would never live to see Nick happy again. She credits you with changing his life."

"Oh, I don't think I changed it – just helped him sort it out and encouraged him to move forward again."

"Well, thanks. Nick's the brother I never had."

MYSTERY SOLVED

August 15, 2002

"That was a delicious dinner, thank you Samantha." Kyle stood to clear the table.

"Wait, we're not finished yet." Samantha headed to the snack cabinet.

"I really can't eat another thing."

She reached inside and retrieved a small, gift-wrapped package. Handing it to Kyle, she kissed him.

"Happy Birthday! Kyle, through the years, I haven't been very receptive to the readings you do. Even though I see the people you help, I never realized the value of it all, until the reading you did for Nick. I'm a believer now in what you do and this is just a small symbol of my support. I'm sorry I didn't acknowledge your ability sooner."

At that exact moment, the phone rang. Kyle answered.

"Hello, may I help you?"

"Hello, Kyle Saint Rouse? I do hope I'm pronouncing that correctly. May I speak with Kyle?"

"This is Kyle."

"Kyle, you don't know me, that is, we've never met. A friend of mine, Stephen Westville, referred me to you. Stephen and I are from the same hometown in Great Britain. I've known him for over 65 years. Stephen mentioned you are in communication with…" he paused. Kyle could hear papers shuffling. "Oh yes, Gladys Osborne Leonard, Mrs. Leonard, is that correct?"

"Yes," was Kyle's short reply, not wanting to put too much forward before he could sort things out.

"Very well. I have been working on a project concerning crop circles for sometime now, 20 years, roughly. Are you familiar with crop circles?"

"No, I'm afraid I know nothing about the subject."

"Good – splendid. Then you won't have an opinion of your own. Crop circles are beautiful designs, some are geometric patterns, others less intricate, but spectacular nonetheless, somehow woven into rapeseed crops. These are happening all over the planet, but the ones we examine are mostly in the U.K. Well, during 20 years of exploring this phenomenon, I have postulated a theory or two and I need your help, Mr. Saint Rouse."

"Please, call me Kyle. I'm sorry, I didn't get your name, sir."

"That's because I am hesitant to tell you, but Stephen assured me you are trustworthy. You see Kyle, it is very important to keep what I am telling you and requesting of you and above all my identity, strictly confidential. No one except Stephen must know I have spoken to you. Do you agree?"

"Certainly, sir." Kyle was intent on listening even more closely now.

"Thank you, Kyle, quite good of you. I am Arthur Stanley. I've worn many hats in my professional career: educator, science advisor, procurer of intelligence. Although I am retired, my colleagues would have a go at me if they found out I had resorted to this sort of thing – reaching out to the dead. But Kyle, I don't for one minute believe in the finality of death. I've seen the research, the hard evidence. Still, all the work around which I've structured a lifetime, all of my credentials, all of my published papers and books would be for naught, if this or any subsequent conversations would be revealed. So I very much appreciate your loyalty, Mr. Saint Rouse, eh, that is Kyle."

"What would you want me to do, Mr. Stanley?"

"First Kyle, I am interested in Mrs. Leonard contacting another in spirit, Sir Oliver Lodge. Have you heard of him?"

"Yes, Mr. Stanley, I have. He was one of Mrs. Leonard's staunchest supporters. I believe he wrote the forward to her autobiography, *My Life in Two Worlds.*

"Well, before that, he was a foremost physicist, world renowned, in fact. He was a legitimate member of academia and an inventor, free thinker and a proponent of life after death. A very daring man for his day, I might add. He wasn't a bit wary to have an open conversation about life on the other side and even published on the subject."

"That's okay, I do understand your concern. So, Mr. Stanley, you want me to contact Gladys… Mrs. Leonard that is… and have her contact Sir Oliver and ask him what exactly?"

"Ah, that's the question. At this time Kyle, there is no reason to tell you what to ask Sir Oliver. We must do some preliminary testing to evaluate if Mrs. Leonard is indeed contacting Sir Oliver. Although she was a commoner and he a member of the upper echelon of the scientific community, perhaps his fondness for her will enable them to communicate.

"I will send you by post – I don't use a computer, everything by post – the way to proceed. I have your address, you'll be hearing from me soon. Thank you, Kyle; I've enjoyed our conversation immensely. Remember, not a word of this to anyone. Good night."

"Thank you for calling, Mr. Stanley. I enjoyed our conversation equally as well. I'll wait to hear from you."

Kyle had no sooner returned the phone to its cradle than Samantha asked, "Well, come on, who was that?"

He hesitated for a moment, inhaling deeply. His right hand traveled worriedly across his head, front to back, while he exhaled fully, and then replied ever so slowly, "You know, I think it was the CIA."

"CIA?" Samantha was puzzled, and then waved off Kyle's reply as a joke. "Just open the gift before you have to leave for work."

"What gift?"

"The gift in your hand!"

With all the mystery of the phone call, Kyle had forgotten about the gift, which he held in his left hand throughout the phone conversation.

"Oh my God, I'm sorry honey. I completely forgot what we were doing."

"I hope you like it."

"When have I not liked something you've given me?"

When Kyle tore through the wrapping paper, Samantha witnessed a wave of expressions transition across his face – first confusion, then shock and disbelief, followed by some sort of sadness.

"Kyle?" she said, to no response. He was examining the gift, a book, first front, and then back, then front again. "Kyle!" she called again, a little more intense this time. As he looked in her direction, she could see tears in his eyes. "What's wrong? It was supposed to make you happy." Kyle reached for a kitchen chair, pulled it away from the table and sat down gingerly.

"This is her," he said barely audible.

"Who?"

"The woman driving the bus all those years ago and the woman mopping the floor, this is her."

"Kyle, what exactly are you talking about?"

It was then he realized just how long-ago a time he was talking about and how cryptic it must have sounded to Samantha.

"Oh, I'm sorry. It's just that it was all so long ago. I was 19 and about ready to be drafted to go to Vietnam, or so I thought. A few months earlier, I had decided to drop out of college because I wasn't doing so well majoring in music. I would have gone, had I been drafted, but I always felt it might have been a one-way trip. Anyway, that was a long time ago and I truly have no regrets. I like the way my life turned out."

"Hey, it's not over yet. What is it with the book? Why so sad?"

"It's the picture on the dust jacket. It's Gladys in her later years. I have never seen her at this age. Well, I guess I have but it was in a dream I had just before I went for my pre-draft physical. I had a dream where a green colored bus pulled up to me." He paused and gazed across the room.

"Yes, I remember, I was standing on a corner and the odd colored bus pulled up and stopped. The door opened. The driver was an elderly woman, this woman." He held up the book facing the picture of Gladys toward Samantha. "She was dressed in Army fatigues. She just smiled at me, closed the bus door and drove off. I didn't understand it at the time but such an odd dream, I couldn't possibly forget that face and smile."

"And the floor? You mentioned something about mopping the floor."

"Yes, yes the floor!" Kyle continued. "I saw her again. It was the day of my physical. Naturally, I was nervous for some time as that day approached." He stopped abruptly. "Oh my God, that's why Gladys appeared in the dream. It was a message to me that the Army was passing me by. So that's what this is all about. I've been getting guidance and encouragement in this lifetime from the other side all along. I never thought of it that w..."

"And the floor?" interrupted Samantha.

"On the day of the physical, at the last examining station, the Army doctor told everyone to bend over. He called for another doctor, tapped me on the shoulder and said to bend over for him. When the other doctor saw my crooked spine, he said no way, they couldn't use me. It was the scoliosis.

"Of course, I was in a hurry to get dressed and get out of there, and in my rush I got disoriented and couldn't find the exit. I spied someone mopping the floor down a deserted hallway, so I went to ask the person the way out. I said 'Excuse me, can you tell me the way out?' When the person turned to face me, it was this woman." He held the book to face Gladys toward Samantha again. "She didn't speak, just pointed down the hallway."

"You didn't try to get her to say something?"

"You have to understand, I didn't realize who she was back then, or that Gladys was a real live person at one time. Anyway, I was so nervous, I just wanted to leave that building. I did turn back, but she was gone. That's right, she was gone and two army officers were walking in my direction, so I took off. My God, Gladys has been with me for so long. Even then, she was so close.

"Anyway, Samantha, thank you for this lovely gift. It turned out to be far better than you thought it would ever be. Let's see, *The Mediumship of Mrs. Leonard* by Susy Smith." He flipped it open. "Hmm, 1964. That's four years before Gladys passed away and five years before I met her. This will be a birthday to remember, what with this book and the call from the CIA." They both laughed and exchanged a kiss, then another.

"Oh, look at the time, I have to shower and get ready for work," Kyle said. And with that, he was off.

＊　＊　＊

"This came for you, Kyle," Samantha said as she gave him a hand-addressed letter, "something from Washington, D.C. Do we know someone there?"

"No, I don't think so." Kyle examined the envelope and then slowly slid a knife under the flap to open it carefully, leaving the return address intact.

"Oh, it's from that man who called the other night. You remember on my birthday, CIA?"

"I thought you were joking about the CIA."

"I was joking, but I do get a sense there is more to him than we know. He does have an office in Washington. I know what you're thinking, Samantha, and no, I will not now or ever research someone I'm reading for. Sorry, I won't do it!"

"Well, what's he say there?" she asked.

"He wants to conduct a preliminary experiment. He wants Gladys to contact Sir Oliver and have him name the title of three books in his Washington office library – what shelves they are on and their position number, i.e. third book from left. This will prove to him that she is connecting with Sir Oliver."

"Oh, is that all?" Samantha said.

"He also asks why I think Gladys talks to me, a postal employee and not to him, a bona fide scholar well ensconced in the scientific community?"

"Well, that pompous ass!" Samantha yelled. "I don't care for him Kyle, he's belittling you. Didn't you mention, when he called, his excessive anxiety about telling anyone he had reached out to you?"

"Yes, he made me promise, not a word to anyone."

"Maybe that's why Gladys doesn't communicate with him. He's not free to speak his own mind, he's always worried what others will think."

"I think he's just desperate. He said he's retired; I think he's looking for answers before he's not here anymore. I'll try my best, but I just can't spend an infinite amount of time on this. We're going back to ten-hour shifts again at work starting Monday for who knows how long."

"Well, what exactly is his title?"

"He was a professor and science advis…."

"That's it," interrupted Samantha. "From now on, he'll be known as the Professor!"

"The Professor – I like it! Tomorrow I'll get working on the Professor's assignment."

Just then the phone rang. Samantha answered and handed it to Kyle.

"It's Stephen from New Jersey," she whispered.

"Hello Stephen, perfect timing," Kyle greeted the man he considered his mentor.

"How's that?"

"I just finished reading a letter from Arthur Stanley. I don't know if I can accommodate him the way he wants."

"I understand Kyle. He did mention he might be contacting you after I had told him about you and Mrs. Leonard. Remember the story you told during class about Mrs. Leonard leading you for years on your spiritual path? I assumed it was true."

"Indeed, it is true."

"I hope you don't mind I told him about you. I wanted to mention it to you, but with Rose's passing, it just slipped my mind. He is a bit of a stickler while reaching a conclusion, but you can be sure of its accuracy. Everything has been methodically considered; there are no flaws. That's the way he works, that's the way he's always been and at 74, I don't see him changing. I hope this sheds a little light on the situation."

"Yes, it certainly does. For 74, he has a good strong voice and plenty of ambition. I have to give him credit."

"Yes, he's such a perfectionist, he'll live forever." They both laughed at that comment. "Kyle, the reason I'm calling is I've decided to start another class next week. After my wife passed, I was so depressed I initially thought I would wait six months, but now I think it would be better to be with people. Rose would want it that way. You know, I see her around me, but only in very short glimpses. So Kyle, are you interested in joining? Many of the others will be here also."

"You bet," Kyle said without a moment's thought, "that is, if I can work it around Mr. Stanley's request." Stephen burst into laughter. Kyle thought maybe he knew more than he let on.

"We all have our Arthur stories. I'll see you next week at class, same night and time as before. Good night Kyle."

"Good night, thank you for calling me." Kyle put down the phone and turned to Samantha.

"Well, another class is forming. I wouldn't miss this

one. It's kind of a show of support for Stephen after losing his wife."

"What's his take on the Professor?"

"Oh, he admits he's a bit kooky, let's say eccentric, but he does get the job done with persistence. I'll do my best and that's that. I'll try before class starts next week."

On the way to work that night, Kyle pondered just how to proceed with the Professor's request.

"Gladys, can you help me with the Professor's request, you know, the book title test?" He had an unusual idea impressed upon him at that moment, along with a mild head buzz. He was sure Gladys was responding.

This is about ego. Time is running out.

"Hmm, what does she mean, time is running out?" He could see the ego idea as being accurate.

When Kyle arrived home, he had wanted to begin the book title experiment but felt so tired and light-headed he decided to lie down and meditate, hoping that would help him feel better. He was familiar with the light-headed feeling and knew something was up. Maybe Gladys was going to transport him to the Professor's office to see the books for himself. How would he remember their titles?

No sooner did he lie down, than he was in a dream state. This dream state was different, though. In it, Kyle seemed more alert, as if participating with full awareness. It wasn't until later, at one of Stephen's classes, that he learned he was having an out-of-body experience, or OBE.

"An OBE, or out-of-body experience, is something we

all experience, but few of us recall," Stephen said. "Most people are familiar with the term astral projection, but the acronym OBE is what we use today. That is when the less dense astral body leaves the physical body and travels elsewhere. It may happen spontaneously as you begin to fall asleep. At those times, if you are aware of what is happening, you probably will go just around the room. If you are not aware and become startled, should you sense the astral and physical separate, your astral body may reenter the physical body with a jerk and jolt you awake. There's never any danger, though. With practice, it is said you can travel instantly anywhere in the astral body."

In Kyle's OBE, he was with a very attractive woman of about 27, which he gauged from the memory of his daughters at that age. She was dressed rather spectacularly in a brown tweed suit made from the finest fabric. The skirt was mid-calf length and hinted at another time and place. The jacket had a medium-wide lapel and flared over her hips, accentuating her extraordinarily narrow waist. This was one of the most beautiful women Kyle had ever seen. He could feel a strong attraction between them and hoped she was feeling the same. Since this visit seemed to be her idea, he was certain she was feeling the same.

Unfortunately, Kyle's mind was blank as to the identity of this woman, although a strong air of familiarity suggested he must have known her well and for some time.

Gladys — I'm Gladys. Take my hand. I want to show you something.

Kyle was beyond words. He should have felt embarrassed for not recognizing Gladys, but he didn't. The love between them was too strong for any other emotion to register. When he took her hand, they were immediately floating in an upright fashion and although the trip they were taking seemed to cover quite a distance, they reached their destination in a moment.

This is where I lived when I began my journey into mediumship, she continued.

It was a brownstone building. Kyle sensed a densely populated surrounding area and thought it to be London. He could see up and down the street. She turned him around.

This is the theater where I performed. It was frightening at first, but always exciting.

Kyle thought everything in this voyage had such rich colors and textures, far better then they ever could have been in life.

It's the fond memories that make the colors so attractive, Kyle. I wanted to share this with you today as we have created so many fond memories together. I always felt your love for me. Indeed, you were always clear with your love. You would actually say "I love you" to me.

His eyes began to tear.

Do you know who taught you to say I love you?

Kyle transferred his first word: *No.*

It was your father.

My father? My father never said I love you to me – never!

I know, I was with you some of that time. But you see, Kyle, that's exactly how he taught you. Of course, it wasn't intentional on his part to teach you or to hurt you. His mother passed away in childbirth along with twin daughters when he was still a toddler. His father couldn't care for him, times were different and he was given away. He never heard about love from his father, either.

You realized the value of hearing the words "I love you" by not hearing them. A devastating way to learn, I must admit, but it is something you turned into a positive situation. You took that empty place in your heart and cultivated enough love to share with your family and people beyond your family, people you hardly know.

I'm sure you played a part in it all, Kyle transferred, having regained his composure. *Gladys, I am deeply grateful.*

Gladys moved closer and kissed Kyle on the cheek. It was the same soft kiss as Hannah's all those years ago.

Why do I feel you are leaving?

We have become one. Our thoughts are connected. She smiled. *You are correct. Our agreement, the one arranged earlier in your life, has been fulfilled. You see, I was a woman without a child. It was my life's only lament and it was keeping me too attached to the physical plane when I entered the world of spirit. Because of this, I was inspired to become a secondary guide to a young person. I asked for someone with a gentle nature, someone lost in loneliness and uncertainty, much like me all those years ago. That's when I found you. You helped me as much as I helped you. Attaining fulfillment doesn't stop with our last breath. I realize now I was mistaken in judging myself to be incomplete without a child. I was wrong in that regard. I am now free from my bond to the physical world, thanks to you.*

I helped lead you on your spiritual path this far. Now others must fulfill their agreements. I will be less of a dominant figure in your journey. I will not be absent though, because it is love that binds us and true love can never be silenced. Think of me as sitting to the side, watching and waiting.

THE POWER OF FORGIVENESS

"How was your day, dear?" Kyle asked Samantha.

Before she could answer, the phone rang. Samantha checked the caller ID screen.

"Professor Alert!"

"Jeepers creepers," was the best Kyle could muster. He wondered what the Professor was going to say about the delay in the book test. He had hoped to have completed the test by now, but he had repeatedly postponed it, always waiting for the right time. He wouldn't dare mention that Gladys was taking a time out, feeling the Professor wouldn't understand. The way he saw it, he was to continue doing what he always did in readings as if Gladys were still there. In Kyle's mind, she would always be there.

"Hello, Kyle speaking."

"Good evening Kyle, this is Arthur Stanley. How are you this fine evening?"

"I am well sir and you?"

"Fine, just fine, thank you."

"You know, Mr. Stanley, I was just going to begin the first experiment in about a half hour. I'm sorry for the delay. Time just has a way of getting away."

"Kyle, if Gladys is unwilling to cooperate or perhaps she is incompetent, we can just go our separate ways. I must still insist on your confidentiality though. It's just that I feel I'm on some sort of abbreviated timetable, if you know what I mean."

Kyle bristled at the notion of Gladys being inept. He thought of what she had transferred a couple of weeks back, when she had mentioned time was running out.

"Yes, Mr. Stanley, I do know what you mean."

"Well, I won't keep you on the phone, Kyle. I'll be looking for your results in the next few days. Remember, not a word to anyone that I called and everything by post."

"Yes, Mr. Stanley, I'll remember, good night."

Kyle apologized to Samantha, "Sorry dear, I really don't want him to keep pressuring me about this experiment, I might as well get it over with right now. I read better on an empty stomach. I'll save my dinner for later."

As he sat in his office, Kyle had no idea how to conduct this test. He retrieved the Professor's letter from the desk drawer. It read:

> Please get three book
> titles, which shelf each is on and
> the position number, i.e. third in
> from left, from Arthur Stanley's
> office at 2400 Virginia Ave. NW,
> Washington, DC 20037

Kyle began. He sat with pen poised over paper, waiting for the three book titles. If ever there was a test to diminish one's confidence, this was it. He thought again of the comment about Gladys and was more offended. He thought too of time running out for the Professor and felt a tiny bit of vindication off in some darker place within himself. Then he realized none of this mattered. The Professor wasn't sent by Gladys. He began laughing.

"What's the big deal?" Kyle said aloud.

Perhaps it was the laughter that moved him from an intense focus to a lesser concentration that made images transfer more easily. At that moment, words and pictures started entering his consciousness. He began writing down each word, phrase or possible title. It wasn't for Kyle to determine the accuracy. That was the Professor's job. When he finished, he transcribed the page of hodgepodge onto his computer, printed it and prepared it for mailing to the Professor.

"Well, that's that, Samantha. So much for the test. I'll probably never hear from the Professor again."

"That would be a stroke of luck," she replied. "I really don't think anything will ever come of it. Just stick to your readings and Stephen's class."

* * *

When Kyle entered Stephen's house, he recognized all the people from the previous class, except two. There were ten in total, including him. The class began in the usual manner. Stephen said aloud a prayer for protection, guidance and intention, but this night he added a verse of tribute for Rose.

Stephen had an unusual way of praying, Kyle noted. He never prayed to God directly but to those in spirit who Kyle assumed were on a higher level than deceased relatives.

Perhaps he was petitioning spirit guides for assistance in the class. Stephen would end each evening's prayer saying "All of this is made possible by the Creator."

"Tonight class," Stephen said, "since all of you have taken my beginner and intermediate courses, we will spend the entire evening connecting with spirit. First, we will reach out to connect with your own guide or guides. As you have been inclined to take this advanced class, I am sure that each of you has more than one guide. It could be your primary spirit guide that shows up or a guide that is with you for a certain period to help you accomplish something on your spiritual journey. I call those secondary guides. Primary, secondary... they're all important, as are all of you. Keep an open mind. You may not see the same spirit person as before. Don't limit yourself to just one. Open up to all possibilities. Now, let us begin."

With that, Stephen started the background music and the breathing exercise to relax everyone. The guided meditation flowed along gently to the part where he said, "Now you are in your sacred sanctuary – your safe place. A door across the way is opening and a person in spirit is coming forward to meet with you. Talk with them. Ask questions. Enjoy the experience."

Some time before, in the very first set of classes, Stephen had mentioned that the idea of the opening door in the guided meditation was really permission for the subconscious to take action and explore the unseen world.

"Although we ask for spirit guides to come through the door," Kyle recalled Stephen saying, "we trust in the plan of guidance for us that whoever comes forward will have a pertinent, useful message. This is my idea of faith, trusting in guidance. Guidance could be the Creator's plan after all. Ask for guidance and give yourself permission to hear it."

The door was opening and a figure was moving toward Kyle. He did not concern himself with whether the person was walking or floating. He had a desperate desire not to disrupt the vision. Finally, the figure stood in front of Kyle. It was a woman. She had a feel of familiarity. He knew this woman, but his mind was blank.

Hello Kyle, it's Rose, Stephen's wife. Do you remember me?

Of course I remember you! But you look much younger and why me? Oh, I'm happy to see you, but Stephen said he never saw you for any duration, just glimpses since your untimely departure.

That is true. Oh, I try throughout every day for Stephen to maintain a vision of me, but he is still too angry because I left so abruptly. Also, he is consumed with guilt that he was warned by you regarding the ill health of someone in the class and never thought of anyone but himself. Tell him I forgive him. Please tell him. He looks on you as the son he never had. Tell him I am here and I forgive him. By the way, it seems we can change our appearance instantly on this side. I chose to look the age when I first met Stephen, when I first knew real happiness.

Suddenly, Kyle's link with Rose was deteriorating. What went wrong?

BOOM! A clap of thunder sounded from out of nowhere. Just moments later, a gusting wind shook the house and torrential rain fell.

"Ah, there go the thunderstorms as promised on the

evening weather forecast," Stephen said. "I thought I might have been thinking something inappropriate and offended someone on the other side." Stephen laughed and the class joined him. Just then, a flash of lightening illuminated the room, quickly followed by another clap of thunder. The lights flickered, then darkness.

"Everyone, please remain seated while I light some candles," Stephen cautioned. "That's one good thing about being involved in metaphysics; there are always candles around." Stephen lit two candles in front of him, then turned around and lit four more spread out behind him.

"I apologize for the interruption. I do believe the excitement has brought everyone back to consciousness. We may have to curtail the class if the lights don't come back in a few minutes, although I won't put you out in this heavy rain. This is rather cozy. Does anyone have any questions while I'm deciding if we shall continue?"

"Yes, Stephen," said one of the new students. "What exactly is a soul group? I've heard that phrase several times recently and have been looking for an explanation."

"There is really quite a bit of reinforcement and assistance that goes into each life in the physical," said Stephen. "A soul group is just that – a group of souls who have desired and agreed to be in the physical at the same time and connected in some way. They probably have been together for several earth lives but in different capacities. They could be family members: one time a son, another time the mother and so on. This is not to suggest they would have to be related every time. Usually a soul group member will play an important role in another group member's life. It could even be a brief but pivotal time, a real turning point. For instance, perhaps your mother's secret lover was a soul group member whose love had given her the assurance she needed in a time of deep, dark despair."

Suddenly, the rain stopped as quickly as it had begun. The power, however, remained off. Stephen ended the class early and asked Kyle to stay a moment longer.

"Now Kyle," Stephen said in the dim of the candlelight, "you don't have to share what happened in your meditation, I realize that some things are private. But I have a deep sense that something of value did happen. I am being told by my spirit guide to dig a little deeper. As the meditation was in progress, I could see a beautiful white light surrounding you, to which I was very attracted."

"You're right, Stephen. When the door opened, out came a woman I didn't recognize at first. It was Rose. I'm sorry, Stephen, if this is unpleasant in any way."

"No, not at all, Kyle. Quite often the spirit person cannot break through the trauma of the surviving loved one."

Kyle thought back to the first demonstration with Simone, when the teenage suicide victim first appeared to his aunt rather than his mother.

"Please continue, Kyle and don't hold anything back."

"Thank you, Stephen. After Rose identified herself, she expressed a deep concern for any anger you may have toward her for passing so unexpectedly. She also wishes to relieve you of your guilt. Rose said she forgives you for not thinking of her health when I emailed you the day after the first class. She forgives you."

"Kyle, I'm so ashamed. I feel as though I let the love of my life slip away. I'm sorry, Rose. I'm sorry I let you down." Stephen slumped into a chair in remorse and began to cry.

Just then the flames of the two candles standing together united and tripled in size. Stephen's attention was drawn to the display. He stood and gasped.

"Rose? Rose? Rose, I can see you!" he cried. "You're here! You're really here! I love you. I miss you so much. Stay with me, if only for a while – please, one last time."

Kyle left Stephen standing in the darkness, crying but not alone.

*   *   *

When Kyle returned from work in the morning, he found a letter from the mail that Samantha had left on the kitchen table. It was from the Professor. Upon first touching the envelope, Kyle noted a feeling of desperation. When he opened the letter, reality concurred. It read:

>Dear Kyle,
>
>I have received your material by US Mail and read it all with interest. The first result regarding the Stanley office was not as clear as one might have

hoped. Try to get a book title from the second floor office in my home, 120 Summer Street, Culpeper, Virginia.

Arthur

"Now this is progress," Kyle laughed aloud. "The Professor is willing to accept just one book title, no mention of shelf and placement." He headed upstairs to bed. He was looking forward to dinner with Samantha so much that he awakened earlier than usual. When Samantha returned home from work, he was already downstairs. She liked that. While they prepared dinner, they discussed the appearance of Rose at class the previous evening.

"It's peculiar from what you've said," Samantha started, "that Rose is aware of what Stephen is mulling over in his mind and maybe even his subconscious. It seems those in spirit have a unique vantage point of life in the physical. Perhaps we could rely on them more, or at least acknowledge their existence and nearness. Just the idea that some part of us continues after we pass is comforting."

"Maybe that's the message I'm supposed to deliver," Kyle said, "the continuity of consciousness and the awareness of the departed. When we cross over, our consciousness continues to exist, but right here. We're still right here, a breath away. The deceased aren't visiting to say goodbye one final time, they're calling," Kyle cupped his hands to his mouth, "Hello, we're still here."

"So many in spirit are interacting with their loved ones in the physical," he continued. "Those in the physical just brush it off as a coincidence and deny the dreams and occurrences that are actually happening. Those living in the physical just aren't receptive because they are unaware any of this is possible."

During dinner, Samantha laughed as Kyle told the story of the Professor's letter. Samantha suggested he just write TELEPHONE BOOK in his next reply and be done with it.

"When I get home tomorrow morning," Kyle said, "I'll do another experiment for the Professor. This one, I'll do my way."

As he sat in the office the next morning contemplating the Professor's experiment, Kyle felt he was being impressed upon to conduct the reading by asking questions aloud. He was willing to accept answers from anyone in the unseen world. He made note of each question and answer. He did not focus on a book title, as the Professor had wanted. When the reading ended his notes simply read:

Date: January 14, 2003
Question: What are crop circles?
Answer: Like a fingerprint to a glass, this is
                 our imprint on the planet.
Question: Is there a message in crop circles?
Answer: Yes, one of beauty, organization and
                 existence beyond.
Question: Would you like to say something else?
Answer: On the farm, May 2003.

Question: What is on the farm?

Answer: Big event. Watch. May 2003.

Kyle never fooled himself into thinking he was anything more than an information gatherer. He processed the notes neatly and mailed them that night on his way to work.

To Kyle's surprise, the Professor sent back an exceptionally speedy reply. It read:

> Dear Kyle,
>
> An interesting experiment.
>
> You and Gladys have set up your
> own test and we will watch for
> the date and place.
>
> Arthur

Because of the letter's briefness, Kyle sensed tones of frustration in the reply, maybe even a touch of anger. It was the last time he heard from the Professor by mail.

LIFE TAKES TIME

August 15, 2003

"Good morning and Happy Birthday, Kyle," Samantha said. "It's a beautiful sunny day on the beach." She pulled on the drapery cord and whisked open the curtains. Sunlight flooded the room. Kyle reluctantly sat up in bed, shielding his eyes from the brightness.

"Thank you, dear," Kyle replied. "I was sleeping so soundly, I forgot we were on vacation. Gee, I love it here! You know, I was just having the strangest dream. I was flying model airplanes with some man I couldn't name, yet it seemed we knew each other fairly well. At least, he seemed to know me well. He knew I had been a music major and he said that math was so intertwined with music. Then he asked me, 'Have you discovered the secrets of the circles yet?' I'm not sure what he was talking about, but the planes were fun, if only in a dream. Maybe he was one of my grandfathers who crossed over before I was born."

"I doubt it," Samantha answered. "They seemed to be from a different era. I don't think they would have had much interest in flying."

"What do you say, breakfast and the beach, sound like a plan?"

"Sounds like a great plan, Kyle."

During breakfast and again on the beach, they

reminisced, as was their custom, about all that had happened since their last birthdays. Kyle recalled that it was on this day, exactly one year ago, that the Professor first contacted him.

"Kyle, do you ever wonder whatever happened to the Professor?"

"Oh, that's not hard to figure out. He didn't like my last reading and probably nothing happened in May like I had foretold."

"It's probably for the best. I never cared for his haughty attitude."

The next few years were occupied with the birth of more grandchildren and the continued juggling of time between Kyle's job and his passion, the unseen world. The thought of Kyle's involvement with the Professor was becoming a distant memory until one day in the early spring of 2007, when he received an email from Stephen. It read:

Hello Kyle,

A bit of bad news, I'm afraid. Sadly, our mutual friend Arthur has crossed over. In fact, he passed a few years back.

Unfortunately, I just found out myself. He had wanted me to relocate to his area after Rose's passing, but I decided against it and we lost contact. I thought he was angry, but here he was gone.

You are certainly someone

his soul would gravitate to.

Keep an open mind, maybe

you'll hear from him. I have

enclosed a link to his obituary.

All the best,

Stephen

P.S. I have remarried and all is well.

Kyle clicked on the link to the obituary of Arthur Stanley. By this time, Samantha had come into the room. He told her why he hadn't heard from the Professor. They were taken aback and saddened by the news. He read the obituary aloud in its entirety. It listed the Professor's many impressive accomplishments. They were both astounded by the very last sentence. It read: Arthur Stanley died May 26, 2003, while flying his remote-controlled model airplanes in the fields at his farm.

"Kyle, I sense you're thinking of contacting the Professor," Samantha mentioned as they prepared dinner that evening.

"Well, it does seem as though he was reaching out to me in that dream on my birthday a few years back. We were at the beach, remember?"

"I remember, but did you forget how condescending and demeaning he was to you and even to Gladys? I just think it's a bad idea to connect with him."

"He probably moved on anyway. It was so long ago, I doubt I could reach him," he said, hoping to placate his wife.

The next afternoon, Kyle got up early with the

intention to connect with the Professor before Samantha arrived home from work. As he settled into his comfortable chair to attempt to make contact, he wondered why the Professor didn't just approach him in the dream and introduce himself. Kyle began with his usual preparations. He asked his support group to assist in bringing forward the spirit of Arthur Stanley. Immediately, he saw the same man from the dream at the beach.

"Kyle, I'm here! I'm here! Lots to share," the man said.

"Great! I thought I would never hear from you again," Kyle said, not sure this was Arthur Stanley. He had never met him in the physical or seen his picture and had no idea what he looked like.

"I was worried neither you, nor anyone else, was going to contact me. I did reach out to you at the beach, lovely place that was. What I was showing you was exactly how I crossed over in May of 2003, just as you had forecast in the last reading you did for me. Only I wasn't expecting to leave that day, you know – die," he whispered.

Now Kyle thought he was getting somewhere. The man had referred to the dream at the beach and the former reading Kyle had done four months before Arthur's passing. Kyle was convinced this was indeed the Professor.

"Oh, sorry, Sir, about that prediction and sorry it took so long to connect with you. I only learned of your passing yesterday."

"Not to worry, it seems time is not an issue on this side. Being dead, as they say, isn't so traumatic either. I see things differently now and I don't have to worry that others will be so critical of my ideas. I can finally be more daring. In a way, I'm more alive now. If only your side would be more attentive."

"So Professor, I mean Mr. Stanley…."

"No, no, Professor is fine," he interrupted, "I know you called me that. It was my cover, after all."

"Cover, Sir?"

"Oh Kyle, you are the comical one! Stephen told me you had picked up the CIA involvement on my very first call to you. That was a very accurate appraisal, but no sooner did you say it, than I'll bet in came a bit of a self-doubt. So your brain made it into a joke. I see this frequently. That's why agents are trained to listen to their first impressions. Don't let the brain make its own story. The brain is good for planning and plotting, not intuition."

"So, you really were CIA?"

"I was MI6, the motherland's CIA, on loan to your country originally because of my specialty."

"What was that, Sir, your specialty?"

"Ancient archaeological mysteries. You never knew? It's all over that Internet rubbish everyone glorifies so. Internet – broke apart so many intimate contacts, it did, but it is perfect for disseminating misinformation.

"Now, as I said. I have a tremendous amount of information to share."

"I'm all ears, Professor."

"No, no, not just yet, Kyle. If we're going to work

together, we have to prioritize. First, you are willing to work with me, to continue the unfinished work from my physical life, to help keep my name alive and prominent in the scientific community, aren't you?"

"Yes, Professor, I am."

"Wonderful! Then you must build an antenna."

"An antenna?"

"Yes, an antenna. You see, the CIA was developing a protocol where anyone could communicate with the dead. They wouldn't have to be naturally sensitive such as you and Stephen. Of course, there was great controversy in our ranks due to the notion that we bury our secrets. My team wanted to move forward with this unprecedented work. Others wanted to abandon the project. In short, I lost and was mandated to tender my retirement. In reality, no one working on a project of this magnitude would be permitted to fade into the sunset of retirement. For five days a week, an agent drove me to an office, where I was banished with the title of consultant. I was under constant scrutiny, even at home. My every keystroke was monitored."

"So that's why everything handwritten and by post."

"Yes, for some reason the agency didn't deem the U.S. Mail relevant. Stephen was kind enough to supply me with a prepaid mobile at our occasional lunches together. Kyle, my wife was devastated. She had battled depression for years, but my confinement in retirement sent her into a downward spiral. I wasn't permitted to tell her the truth about the project or that my detainment was involuntary. She died thinking I had chosen the agency over her. After her passing, I was ruined, guilt-ridden. My health waned. Seeing this, the agency rescinded my obligations, except absolute secrecy.

"I regret wasting so much of my wife's life by demanding she wait home for me while I was off on some official junket. I thought she'd be here to greet me when I crossed over, but I suppose she'd had enough of me. I do miss her so. She always said if I didn't change, I would end up being alone and well, I suppose she was right.

"Oh, sorry Kyle, I'm just spilling my heart out and it's really not your concern. It's just that you're the only link to a life I once had. Clearly, I would abandon all of this science for another chance with my dear Dahlia. I am truly sorry."

"Why don't you ask for another chance?"

"Ask who?"

"I receive plenty of guidance from your side. Perhaps with your expression of remorse, there's guidance there for you also. Anyway, no apology to me is necessary. I understand better now. Should we continue?"

"Yes, let us continue. You see Kyle, the antenna I was developing never made it off the drawing board. When I heard you were in communication with Mrs. Leonard, who was fully vetted by Sir Oliver Lodge during their time together on the earth plane, I jumped at the opportunity to continue my work, through you, away from the purview of Langley. I thought Sir Oliver, a man of science, could help clear up certain anomalies of the antenna.

"But an antenna, Professor? I don't have room for an

antenna."

"Oh, it won't look like an antenna. It must be shaped like a pyramid. We believe pyramids are what the ancients used to communicate. To whom, we don't know for sure. The inner group I worked with was convinced the ancients were much more advanced than generally thought. The upper portions of their pyramids were covered with gold, which we think served as a subtle energy conductor. Naturally found within the stone were varying crystal formations. Each crystal group has a unique frequency signature. We know that each person has a unique spiritual frequency signature. It seems we build our own frequency signature by our thoughts and actions while in the physical.

If my theory is correct, we may be able to duplicate the pyramid communication with simple means. The various frequency signatures of the crystals should align with the frequency signatures of the departed. Once the antenna receives the signal, it will be simple to convert it to audible sound, much like the crystal radio of yesteryear.

"Why crop circles? What's their part?"

"I believe some crop circles contain clues to identify which crystals to use to communicate with the other side. Edison may be responsible for some of the circles. He was working on a communication device to the spirit world for some time before his demise."

"You mentioned gold. You know I can't afford gold, Professor."

"Build a pyramid from copper tubing, that's an

affordable conductor. It doesn't have to be solid, just the perimeter; four triangles connected. You can construct it to fit your whole body or just the upper body. Obtain an assortment of crystals, but not the black onyx. I must caution you, never use the black onyx."

"Are you sure this is going to work, Professor?"

"Kyle, we'll only be certain when we test it. While you're busy with the antenna, I'll ask for a new chance with my wife. Are you confident asking will work?"

"Professor, you'll only be certain when you test it," Kyle replied. "Just ask."

"Fine, Kyle, I will ask. When you're ready, ring me up and we'll go from there. Good bye for now."

Kyle decided to build the smaller version and wanted the Professor to know he was serious about working with him, so he began the project without first talking with Samantha. In the home remodeling store, he found a roll of soft-coil refrigeration copper. It was 50 feet in total, packaged neatly, taking up very little space and weighing less than 10 pounds. When he got home, he was able to slide it under their bed, out of sight.

He went online to search for crystals. To his surprise, the number of sites was limitless.

He ordered a variety pack of crystals from a website offering free express shipping.

Two days later, when Kyle arrived home from work, Samantha's car was still in the driveway. He rushed into the house to find her in the living room waiting for him. Two packed suitcases were in the middle of the room, along with the coil of copper.

"What's happening?" Kyle asked anxiously.

"That's what I'd like to know!" Samantha answered, her voice filled with anxiety. "Important things first. Mattie called earlier and had just returned home from a night at the hospital. She thought she was in labor. The doctor assured her she wasn't, but insisted she remain in bed the last three weeks of her pregnancy. I cleared it with my office and I'm heading over there to stay with her until the baby arrives so Jared can save his time off for when the baby comes. At least that was my initial plan. Can you explain this?" She pointed to the coil of copper. "I found it under the bed while I was getting the suitcases."

"Oh that," Kyle hesitated, "I spoke with the Professor and he wants me to build a communication device."

"Wait, you contacted the Professor? You know how I feel about him. He's controlling with an inflated ego. In the end, there's nothing there but loneliness."

"That's odd, his wife said the same."

"Whatever. Listen, do what you want, but I'm telling you this: I'm going to Mattie's to care for my daughter for the next three weeks. If you don't come to your senses, I may not be back!" She wheeled her bags to the door and was gone.

Kyle was shocked. He had never seen Samantha this angry in all their years together. Her reaction to his reaching out to the Professor seemed a bit excessive. He felt there was something more to this story. Perhaps, on a subconscious level, her intuition was sensing an event coming that would warrant such anger and transferring it to this situation with the Professor.

In times of great stress such as this, Kyle knew what to expect from his body. He went upstairs and readied himself for bed, waiting for the great wave of emotional exhaustion that would come over him and take him away from the sadness of the moment into a deep sleep. When he woke up, possibly he would have the answer.

"I've been lying here for two hours and I'm still not tired. I know what will help." He found himself at the liquor cabinet, reaching for the Scotch. He poured a generous double over ice with just a splash of water.

Then the doorbell rang. No one was there, but a box sat on the welcome mat as a delivery truck drove away.

"Oh, the crystals!"

He thought of Samantha as he opened the box. His sips of the Scotch turned to gulps. He poured another double. His head began to throb. The crystals were beautiful in an understated sort of way – rose, green, clear, amber and black. He put the crystals in his shirt pocket. As he walked back to bed, he spied the coil of copper and took it to the office. There, he was overcome with curiosity. Sitting on the floor, he began to unroll the pliable material. He held the end of the roll, stretched his arm above his head and with the other hand, made a 90-degree bend closest to the floor. He stretched an equal length parallel to the floor, made a bend and yet another stretch above his head; a triangle was formed. He repeated this maneuver three additional times.

"Voila! A modern-day pyramid for the Professor." He finished his drink and crawled inside the pyramid.

"Professor? Professor, are you there?"

Suddenly Kyle's head began to vibrate similar to the way it did before one of his spiritual encounters, only more profound. It was quickly becoming unbearable.

"Professor!"

The wave of vibrations grew stronger. He wasn't sure he could take anymore, but he was somehow paralyzed within the contraption. He could see inside the top of his shirt pocket. The black onyx seemed to glare up at him. The vibrations intensified. The top of his head was about to explode.

"Help me Gladys! Jeane! Hannah!" Kyle's eyes closed. "Samantha, I'm sorry." He began to fall backward. As he did, the pyramid toppled over and fell away from him, freeing him from its spell.

* * *

The ringing seemed endless and annoying. Kyle reached for his alarm to turn it off, only to realize it was the phone ringing. Still in a haze from sleeping, he managed a soft "Hello."

"Kyle, something's wrong!" It was Samantha. "Mattie was rushed to the hospital. Come as quickly as you can."

"I'll be right there. I miss you," he said before realizing she had hung up.

He dressed hurriedly and headed toward the door, stepping over the coil of copper still on the living room floor. As he left the house, he noticed a small box on the welcome mat.

"Oh, the crystals." They were of no concern now.

In the car, he recalled having the strangest dream just a short time ago, something about the Professor, a pyramid and drinking Scotch. However, Kyle had become alcohol intolerant three years ago. The slightest drink would cause his face to break out in hives.

"It all seemed so real," he mumbled. He glanced in the rearview mirror. No facial distortion. He had an immense longing to see Samantha. He tried calling, but her phone was off.

As he approached the labor and delivery unit, he noticed an ominous feeling rising within him. At the nurses' station, he asked for the whereabouts of Mattie Sojourn, his stepdaughter.

"Please follow me," the nurse replied. She took Kyle to an empty room and said to wait. A moment later, Samantha came into the room. She had tears in her eyes and Kyle knew they were not tears of joy. Kyle opened his arms with a silent invitation. Samantha fell into his embrace.

"The baby's stillborn. He never made it," she cried.

"No!" Kyle whispered. "Is Mattie okay?"

"As well as you would expect. She's in shock and blaming herself."

"Can we see her?"

"In a few minutes, they'll let us in. Mattie and Jared have asked for an hour alone. All the information I have so far has been from the doctor."

"I'm so sorry," Kyle said. "I'm sorry, Samantha, for our differences also."

"I'm sorry too. Listen, it's fine if you want to help people with your readings and it's okay if you want to connect with the other side. Just remember that life in the physical is for us living in the physical. Don't forget about me and my love waiting for you right here, right now."

Her words "my love waiting for you" struck a nerve within Kyle. He thought of the Professor's regret in keeping his wife waiting all those years. Her embers of love were neglected until they burned no more.

The nurse entered and said it was time. She led them out of the small room into a recovery room. There they saw Mattie, Jared and the baby. Kyle and Samantha simultaneously said, "We're so sorry."

Samantha positioned herself at the head of the bed and began stroking Mattie's hair in a consoling fashion. The baby was lying on his mother's tummy, looking much like any other newborn. Kyle asked if he could hold their baby.

"Yes, of course." Mattie offered the baby to him. "Take as much time as you want. The doctor said we could stay here as long as we need."

Kyle cradled the newborn in his arms and could feel the warmth of the baby, probably imparted from the mother's womb, through the blankets wrapped around him. Other than his darkened lips, he looked and felt like any of their other grandchildren at birth.

"What is his name?"

"John – his name is John," Mattie answered and then broke into a torrent of tears.

Kyle held John close, desperately trying to preserve the warmth. He thought it to be John's solitary statement – I was here, if only for a moment.

Kyle began to feel pressure building in the front of his head. He knew this was more than a random tragedy. He looked around the room. Time seemed to be frozen. Mattie's tears were defying gravity. Samantha's outstretched arm was poised, melded to Mattie's head. Jared stared blankly at his wife. The nurse was crouched by the incubator, looking much like a photo as she reached to unplug the power. The only sound was the clock ticking down the seconds and that gave way to a lone angelic voice singing, seemingly audible to Kyle alone.

Kyle's attention was drawn to the blank wall before him. He could clearly see his spiritual support group, usually forgotten at times of such gravity. His support group parted to reveal a woman in white, the woman that had eluded him for so many years. She mirrored Kyle in the fact that she too was holding an infant, only her child was apparently living. She began to speak.

"Do not be forsaken, for this too is the human experience. Even the hardest of times are with reason." She moved her infant's knit cap up the left side of his head and

Kyle did likewise. Through John's light brown hair, Kyle could see a red birthmark resembling a miniature heart. The woman leaned to stand the baby on the floor and as she did, he instantly matured into a young adult. He turned, walked away and vanished. Marcel stepped forward.

"What should happen when one asks for a change to a life plan? Should we deny that person? We are forbidden; we are bound. Remember this day. This soul will return." Marcel stepped aside for the woman in white again.

"Humankind has grown unaware of their connection to the world of spirit," she said. "Together we are in union with the Creator. Apart, we are not. Mankind must reawaken to the guiding light of origin, the once magnificent partnership between physical and spirit. Reunite with those in spirit. Only then will true guidance resonate. This is the plan of providence, of the Creator. This is the message."

Then the woman in white and Kyle's support group vanished. Kyle cradled the baby closer in his arms. John's body was cold. The awe that was suppressing any emotional response had dissipated and was replaced with overwhelming sorrow. Tears pooled in Kyle's eyes.

Kyle recalled the image of the one in spirit walking away from the woman in white. "If you can hear me," he said, "I honor your decision, for whatever reason. You have my attempt at understanding, and if needed, my forgiveness. Perhaps we'll meet again." Then he thought this day would become a marker of time to his family. Future memories would be referenced as before or after John's birth. As such, it was a fresh start of sorts and Kyle mentally asked for forgiveness from all those he had offended in the past and extended forgiveness to anyone who ever hurt him. All indiscretions were forgiven; the slate was clean.

Kyle sensed another in spirit standing before him. He strained to see through his tears.

"Dad – is that you?" Kyle asked.

"Kyle, I am here and have been with you since I passed, but the rapport we had while we were together in the physical and the way you remember me prevented you from feeling me near. That was my biggest regret when I crossed over, how our relationship suffered because of me. I want to apologize.

"Kyle, I'm sorry for being so hard on you, for being so devoid of emotion. I was the one lacking, never you. Because of your deep sense of responsibility and our misunderstanding of your heightened awareness, you felt my sense of desperation in this world and thought it to be yours. It was always my inadequacy you were feeling, never your own and I am truly sorry.

"You travelled a path that I never could have taken you. I'm proud of you." The man paused and his whole demeanor changed. A broad smile brightened his somber face.

"Kyle, I love you."

"I love you too, Dad."

With that, the vision of his father vanished and the activity in the room resumed after what seemed to be a suspension of time.

IT'S TIME TO TELL THE OTHERS

"Kyle, phone for you," Samantha called up the stairs.

"Thanks dear. Hello, Kyle speaking."

"Hello Kyle, this is Stephen. Great news! I've been invited to teach the beginners' class of my metaphysical course at the community college in September. It's a noncredit adult evening class. The class size should be at least double what I'm used to. I'm wondering, would you care to teach along side me? I know you're busy, but I'm being directed very clearly by spirit to ask you."

"Very exciting, Stephen. Tell me more."

"I find it's the best way to advance my spiritual path, by bringing awareness to others one small group at a time. You know, Kyle, having derived my income as a photographer, I have always been free to speak about the metaphysical without fear of repudiation to my livelihood. You as a postal worker, especially at this time of your life, are in a similar situation. We have no fear of being ostracized, unlike Arthur."

"Stephen, I'll do it!"

"Great! I'll email you my ideas. After you look at them, call me. Thanks again, Kyle."

Kyle went to tell Samantha.

"It's a noncredit course at the community college near Stephen's house," he said, "beginning in September and he asked me to teach with him."

"Sounds good, Kyle. You may even see me in the

class."

*   *   *

"It sure is nice to have you along, Samantha," Kyle said as he drove to his first class as a teacher in the fall of 2008. "I'd be a nervous wreck by myself with all this backed up traffic."

"I'm glad to be here. It's taking my mind off of Mattie's due date tomorrow."

"I had the strangest dream last night. It was the Professor showing me he had reunited with his wife. She was there holding his hand as they sat on a sun-drenched beach, much like us."

"Did he say anything?"

"Yes, and it was peculiar, as you might expect. He said the quest for fame was for the physical world. It masks insecurities. This time, he's choosing love. His wife agreed to another go-round."

Traffic inched forward as they approached the street on the perimeter of the college.

"I wonder what the hold up is," Samantha said, "and what's with all these police?"

Just then, her cell phone rang.

"It's Mattie! I'll put her on speaker. Hello, how is everything?"

"Congratulations, Grandmom! It's a beautiful girl, perfect in every way. Jared and I are fine also."

"Oh, thank God! We're so happy for all of you. What's

her name?"

"Well, we may have lost John but we never lost hope. We named her Hope."

"Oh, that's beautiful," cooed Samantha.

"One more thing, she has the tiniest birthmark in the shape of a heart on the back of her neck, just at the hairline."

"Now, how about that," said Kyle.

"Well, gotta go, time for a feeding. Love you both."

Their car was approaching a college security officer. Kyle lowered the window. "Excuse me, officer, what seems to be the problem?" He observed that the officer looked to be about his age.

"It's just some students having a demonstration about the wars going on and voting for change in the upcoming election. Everything is under control at this time, but with the first night of evening classes, the crowd is large. I haven't seen anything like this since my college days back in the Vietnam era."

"Ask him where the Health Sciences Building is," Samantha urged, "that's where we're going."

"Can you tell me where the Health Sciences Building is?"

"You're in luck. It's right here. This is the back of the building. Parking though, is on the other side of the campus."

"Samantha," Kyle said, "I'll let you off here and I'll park the car. You know the classroom number, 319. Tell Stephen I'm on my way."

Samantha left the car while telling Kyle to be careful in

the crowd. He steered the car away from the campus to avoid the traffic congestion. He could reach the other side of the campus quicker using the residential streets surrounding the college. Finally, Kyle reached the parking lot. He took a moment to reflect on Hope's birthmark and what the security officer had dredged up from his memory – Vietnam and college days.

By this time, the protestors were within earshot.

"No more war! Vote for change! End it now!"

"No more war! Vote for change! End it now!"

The evening air was crisp and fresh. An ice cream truck was parked by the lot's exit. Signs of life were all around. Across the street, sitting under a sprawling tree on the lawn of a college building, were two students locked in a kiss. Beyond them, two more students were seated at opposite ends of a board game. Kyle thought of Hannah and him back at the beginning of it all, so very long ago.

Kyle looked to the heavens and mentally said to his spiritual support group –

I know you're here. It's been a long journey. Thank you for your love. Thank you for your guidance. It's time to tell the others.

Then, taking a deep, confident breath, Kyle began his cross-campus dash.

He loved this day. He loved most days.

www.ingramcontent.com/pod-product-compliance
Lightning Source LLC
LaVergne TN
LVHW051405080426
835508LV00022B/2980